S P A C E

SPACE

1st Edition, published by Highpoint Life.

For information write to info@highpointpubs.com

www.highpointlifebooks.com

First Edition
ISBN: 978-0-9861585-4-4

Library of Congress Control Number: 2015940559

ISBN: 978-0-9861585-4-4 (hardbound)

Cover and Interior Design by Sarah M. Clarehart

10 9 8 7 6 5 4 3 2 1

S P A C E

Poems by Bartholomew John Erbach

Photographs by Sarah M. Clarehart

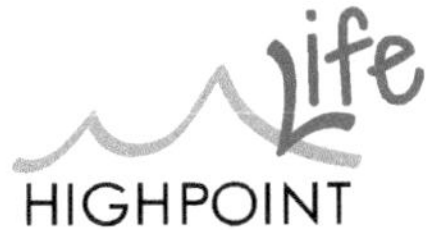

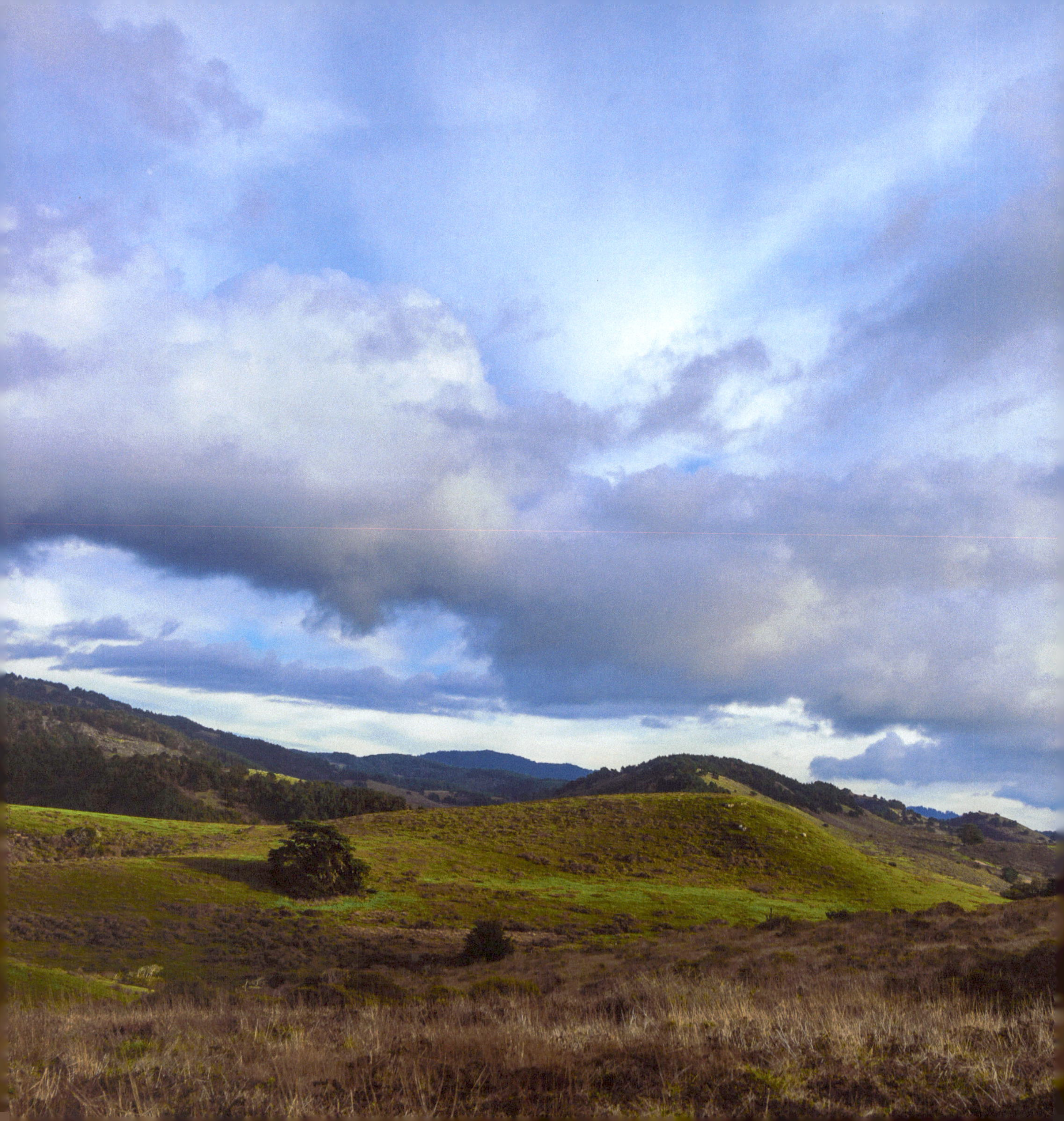

DEDICATION

For my sons

Timothy Paul, the poet

John Nathaniel, the photographer

Who inspire me

More than they will ever know

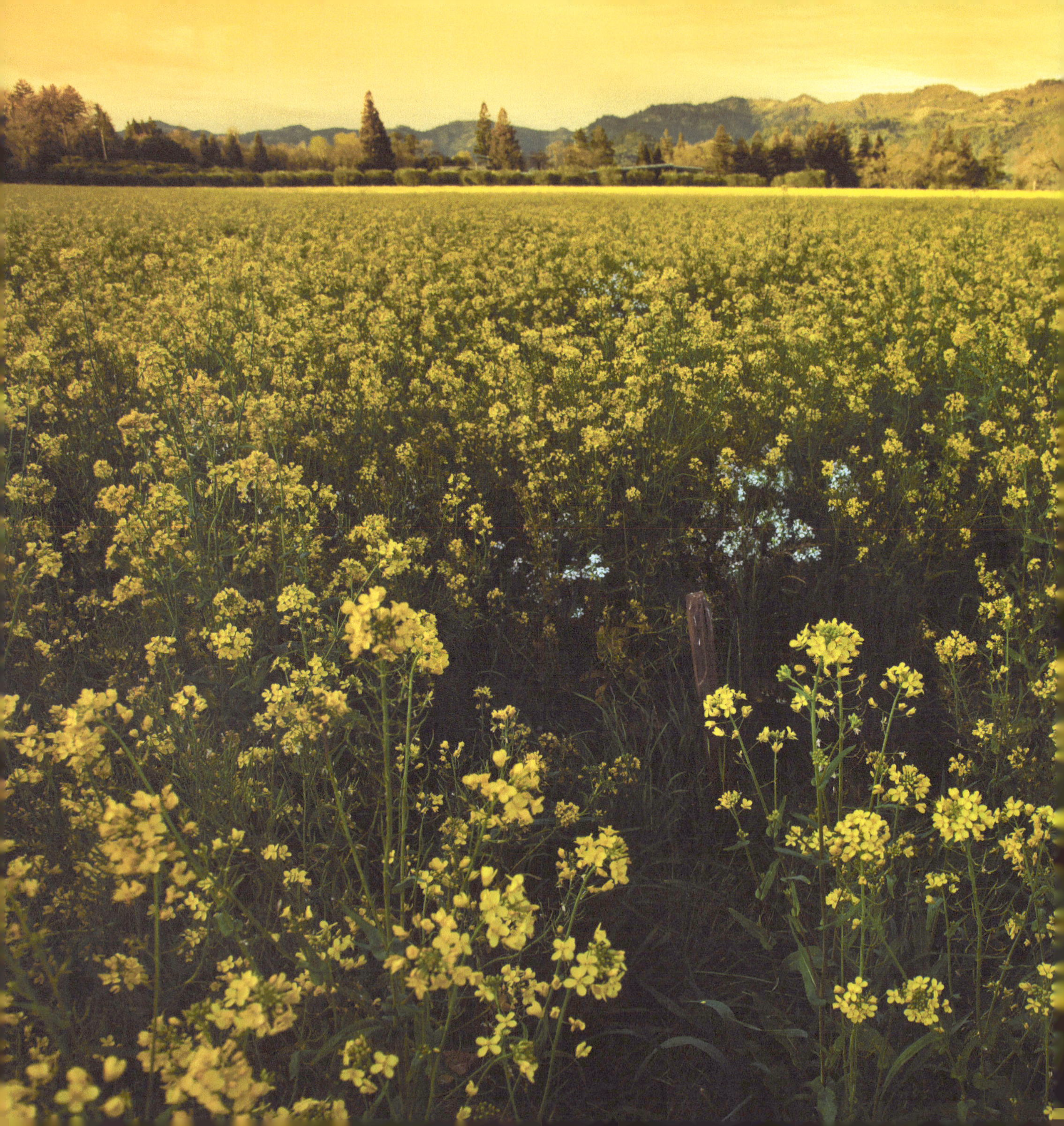

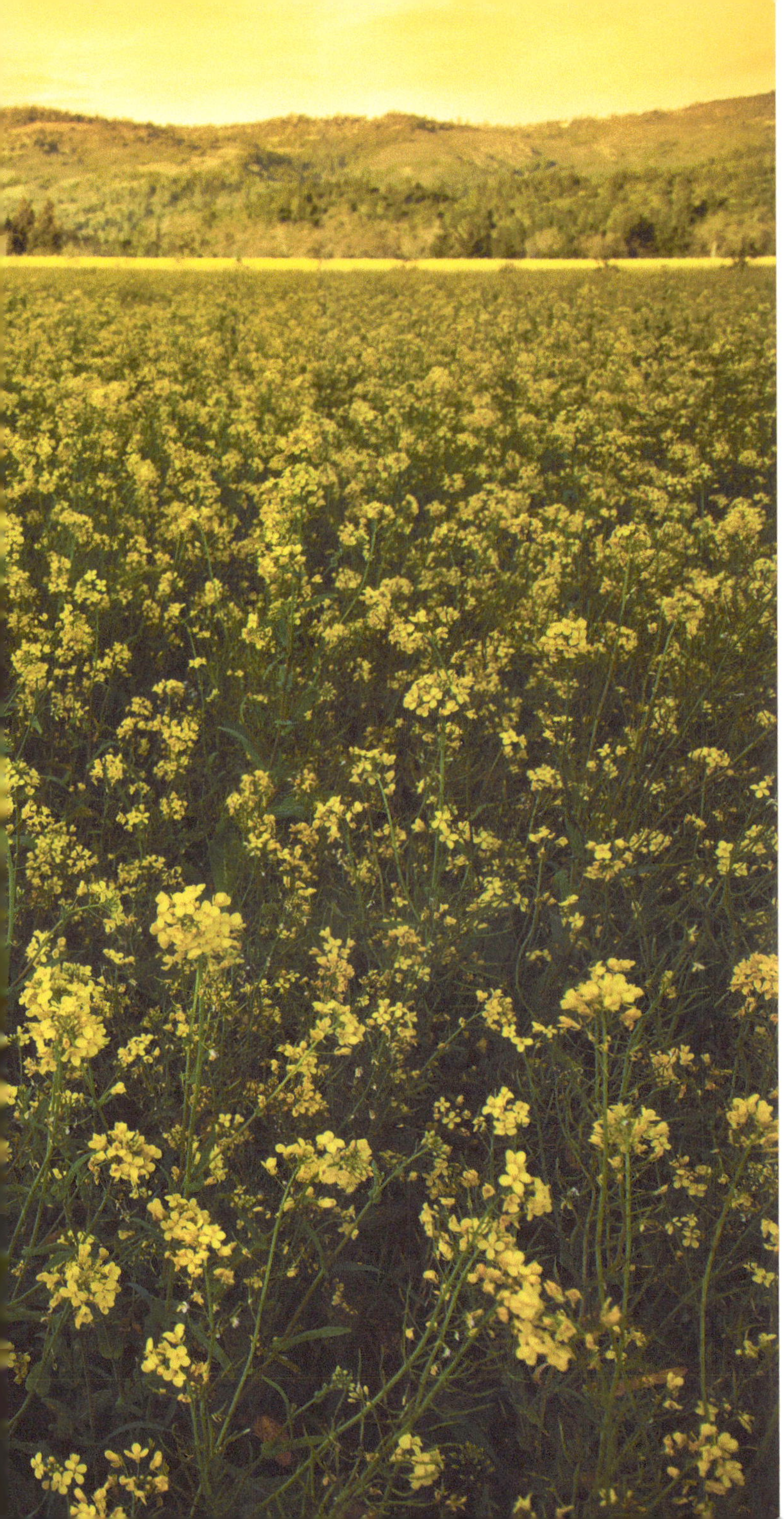

CONTENTS

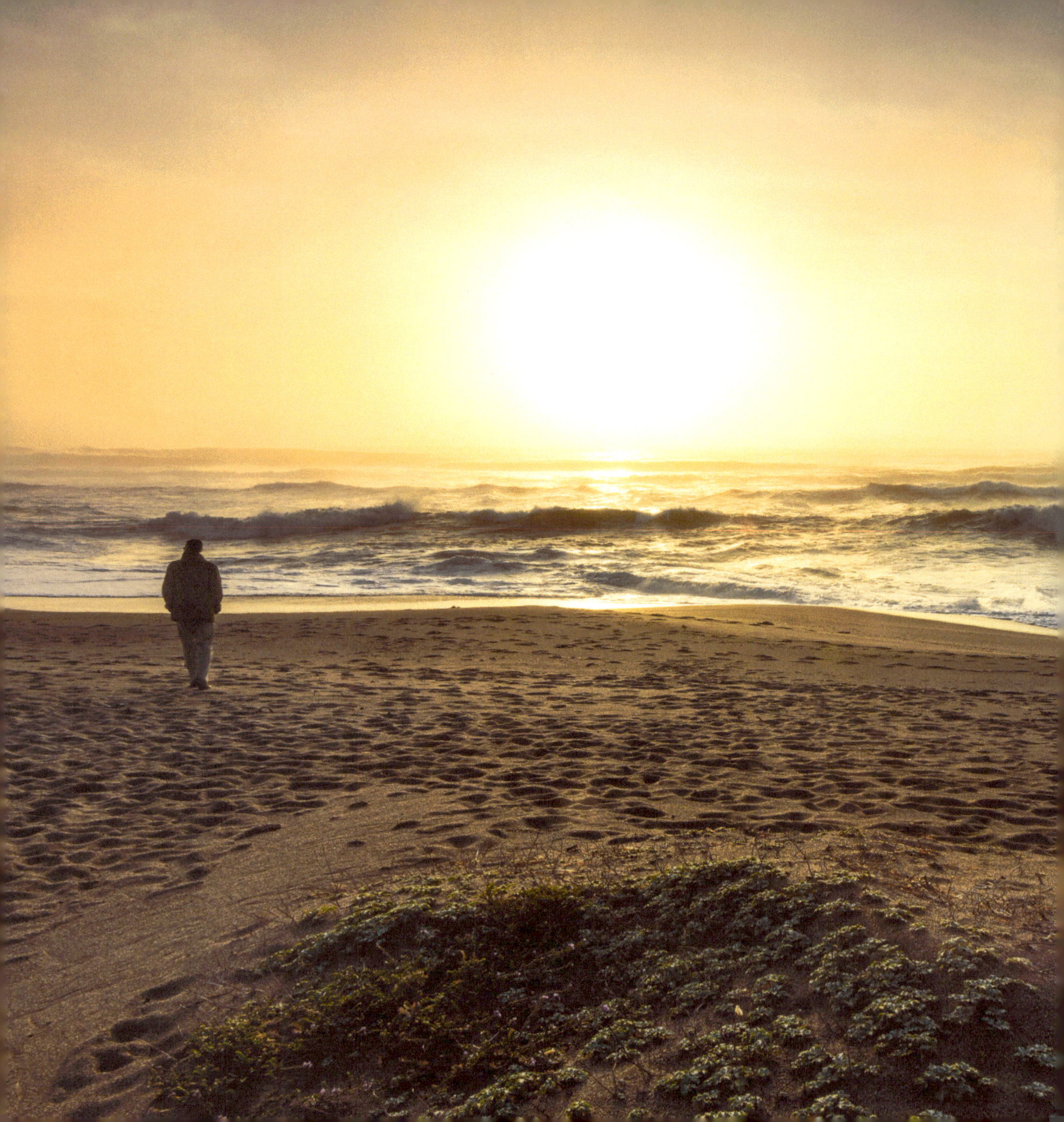

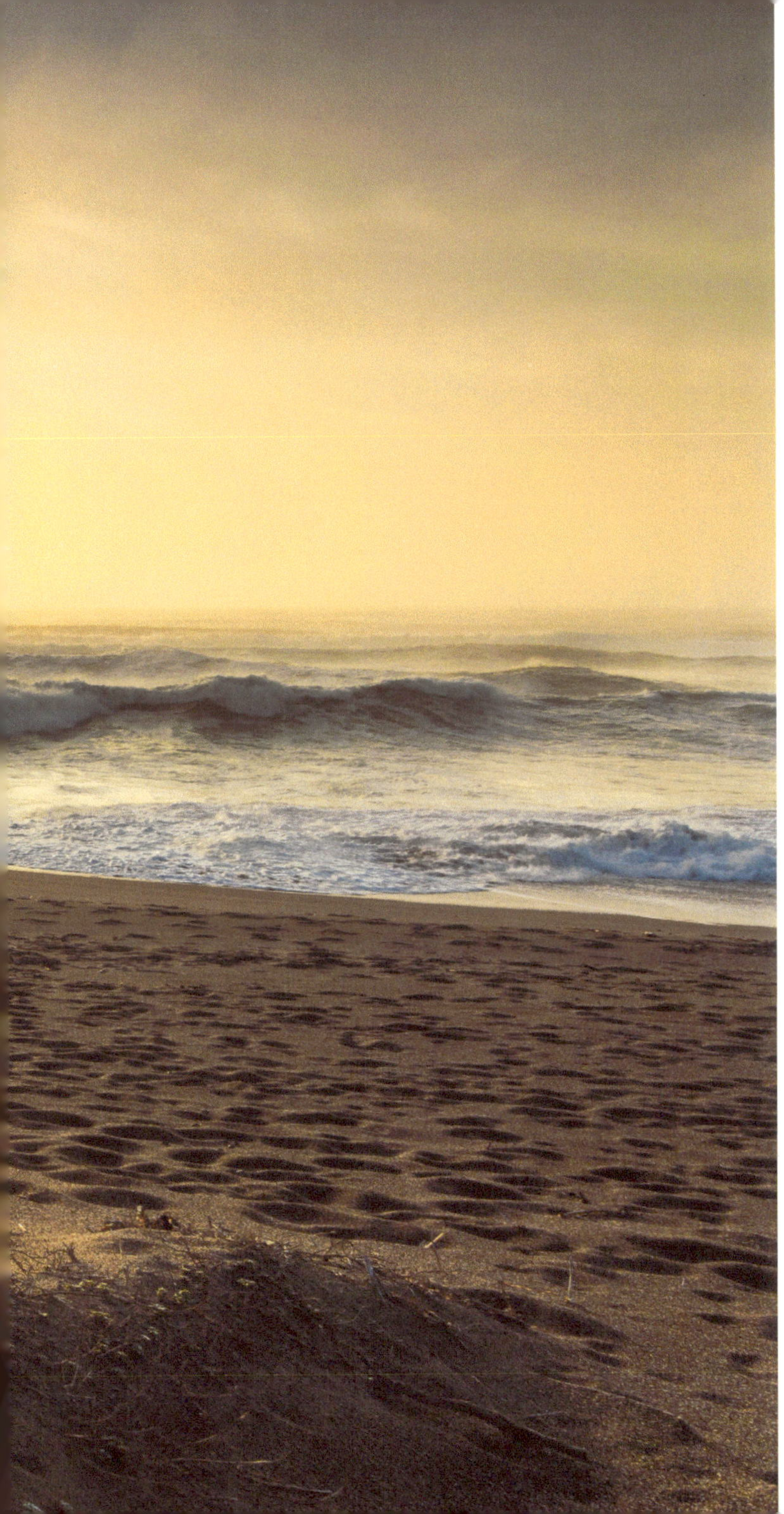

SPACE

There is space for me
Space to stretch out
On this bed and write

There is space in this song
To dream between the sounds

There is space in this body
To wear away rough edges
With gentle ocean waves

There is space in outer space
For galaxies to crash and smash
To die and to be reborn

There is space in our love
To spark another life
With the gentlest touch
Or the kindest word

There is space in my quiet screams
To just let go and laugh
Like a little boy in a sand box

So much space

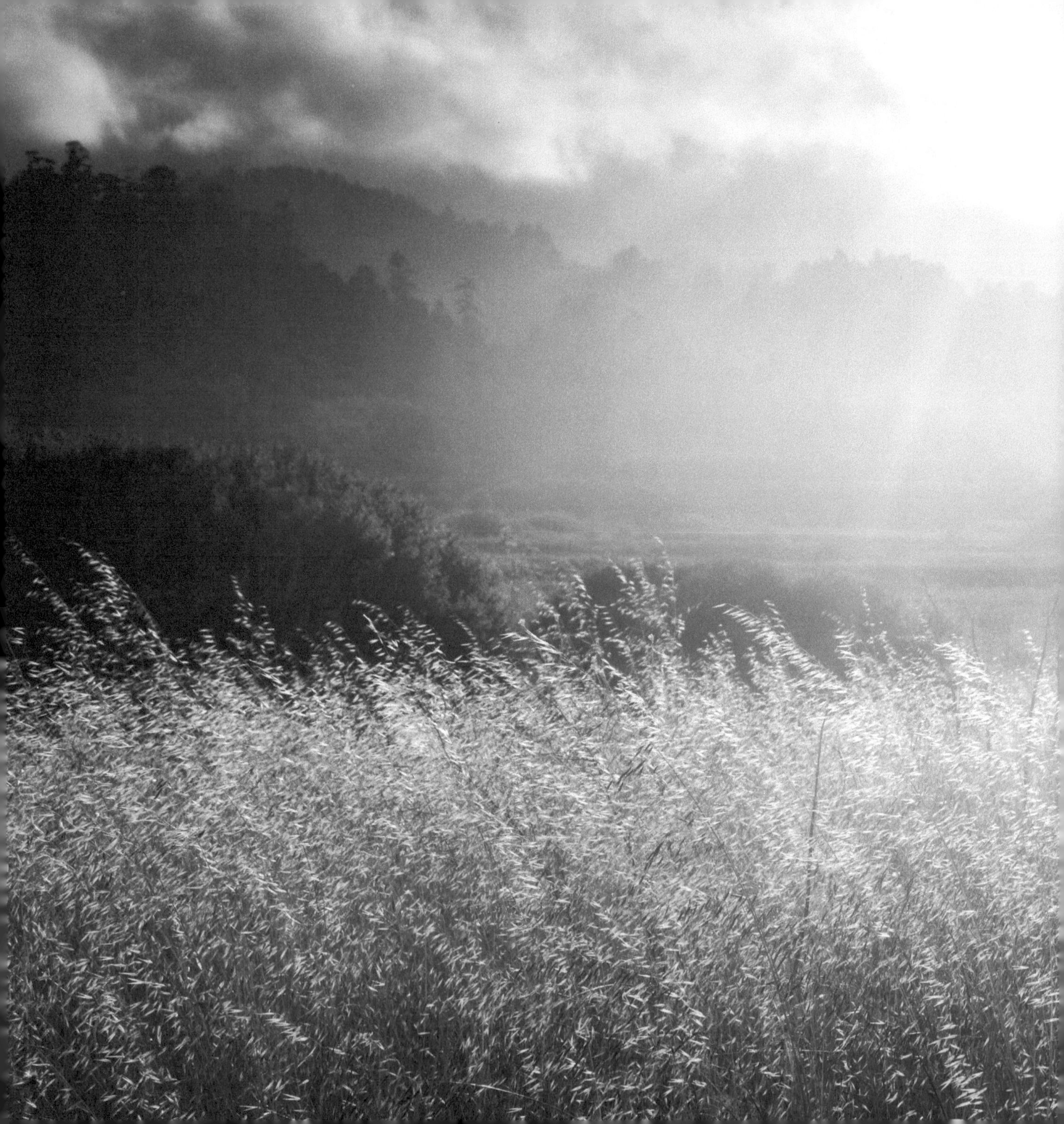

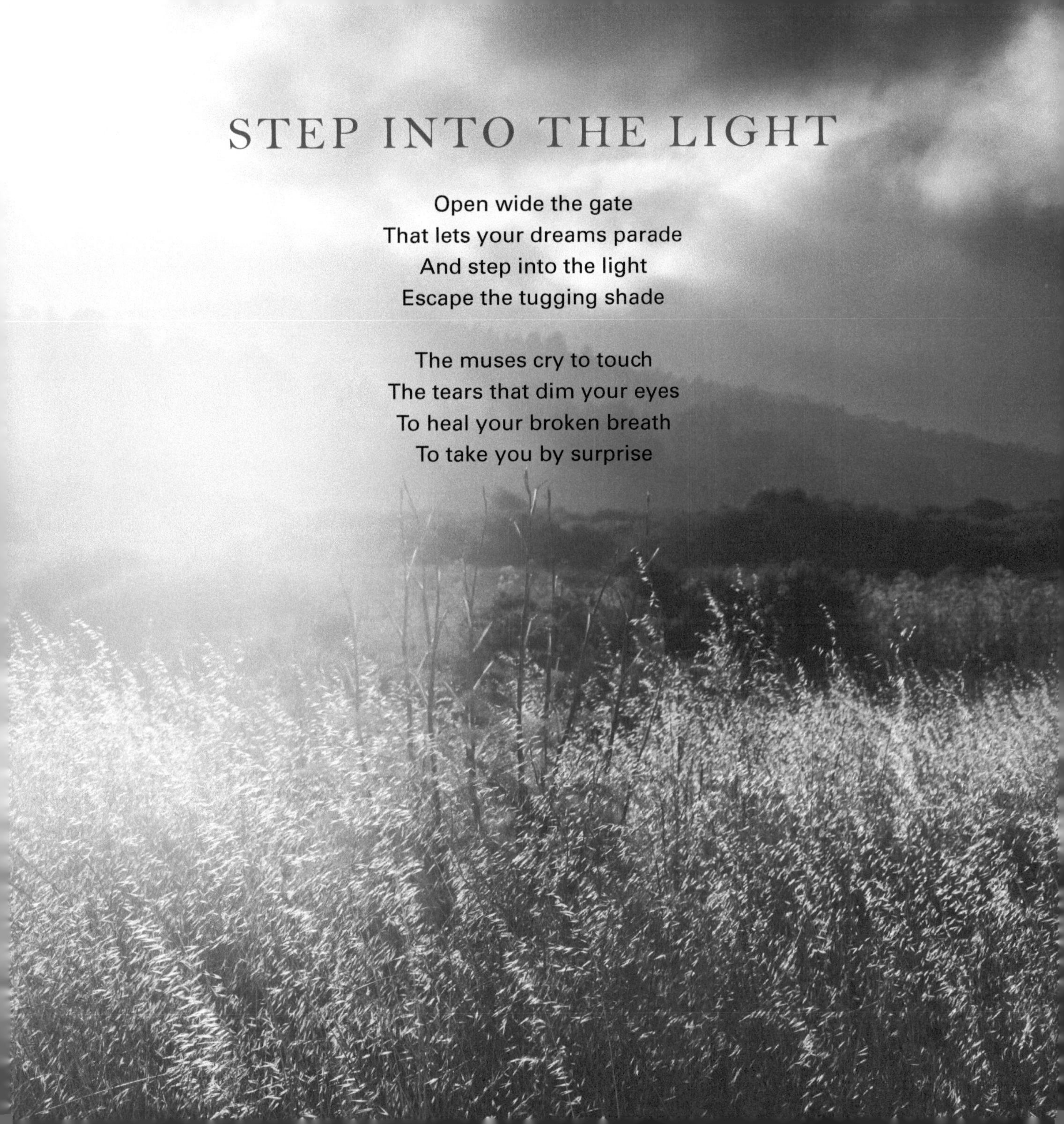

STEP INTO THE LIGHT

Open wide the gate
That lets your dreams parade
And step into the light
Escape the tugging shade

The muses cry to touch
The tears that dim your eyes
To heal your broken breath
To take you by surprise

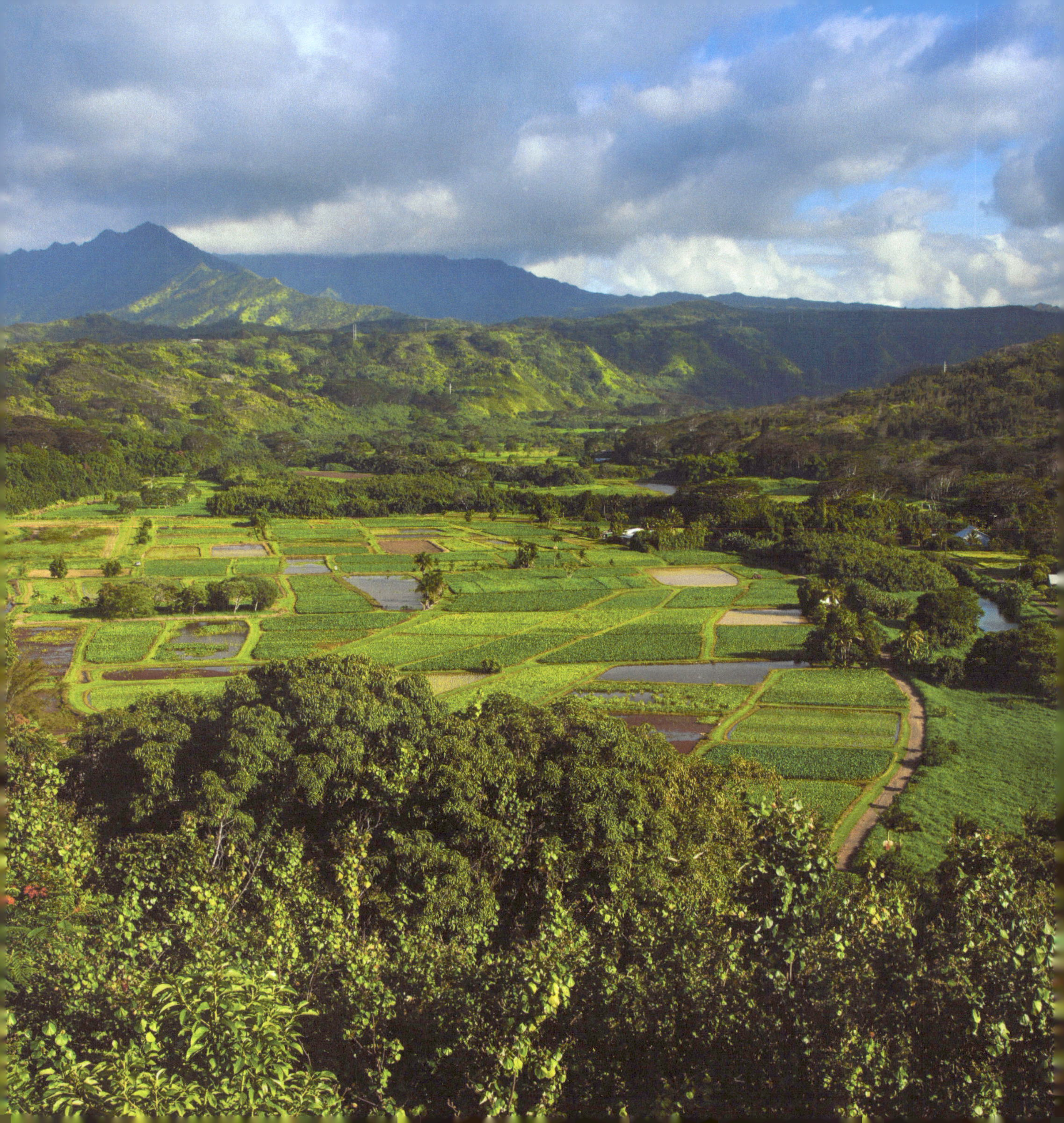

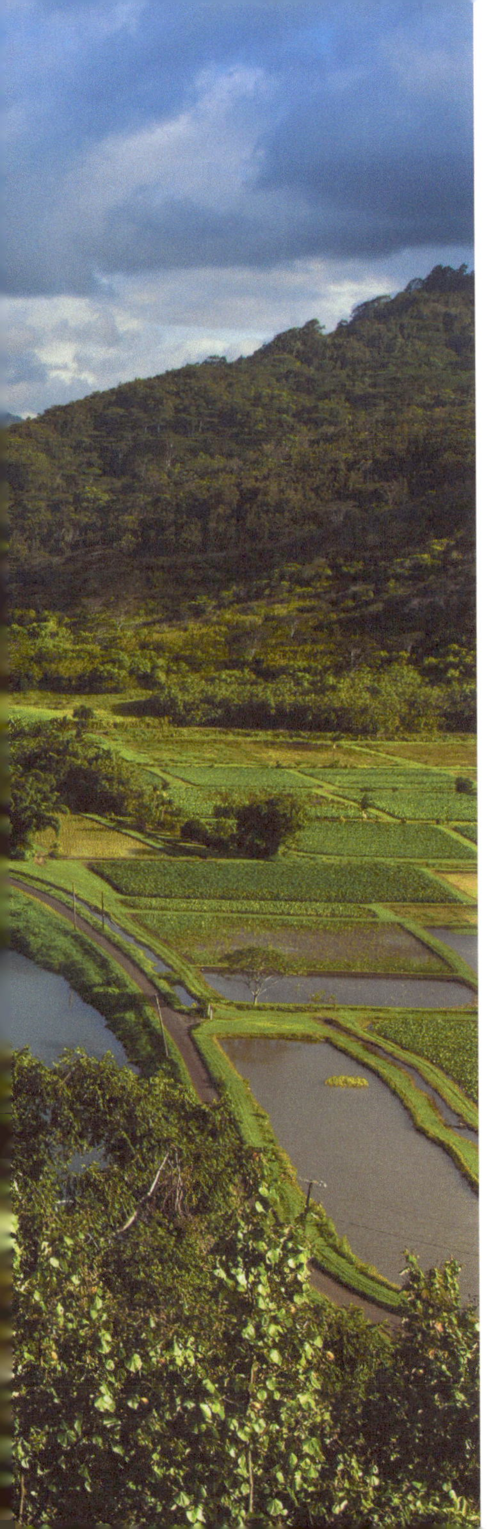

THIS GREAT MYSTERY

Seven hawks swirl
As I drift slowly
Down to earth
Hiking up to
North Lookout

Fields of farms
Flow past rivers of rocks
As cloud shadows crawl
Slowly through the valley

Dusk
So imprecise a word
Filters this day
That slips to night

And so September ends
So quietly
With no one but you to notice
The way I sense
This Great Mystery

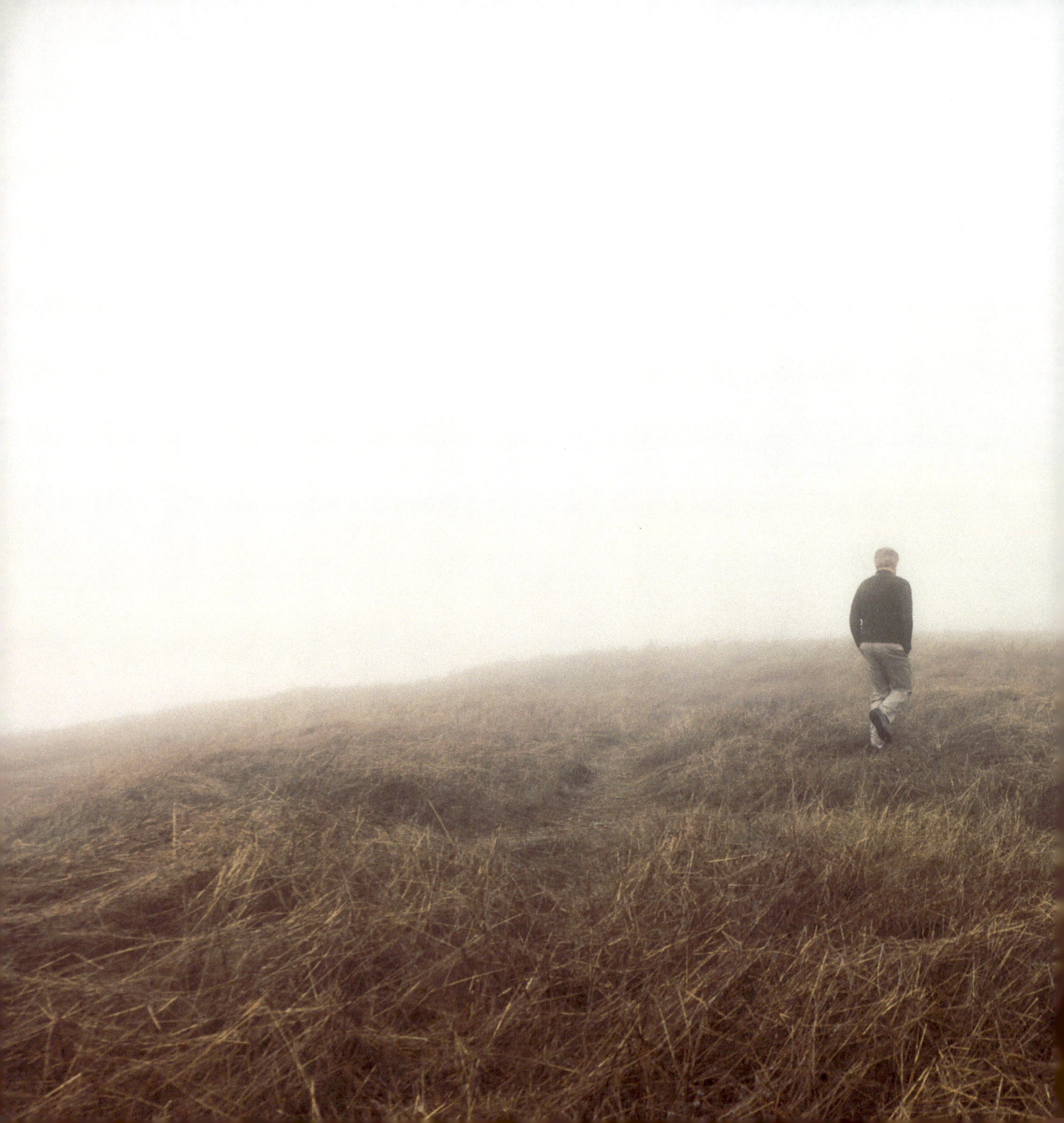

FEED THE WORLD

I feed the world
But starve myself

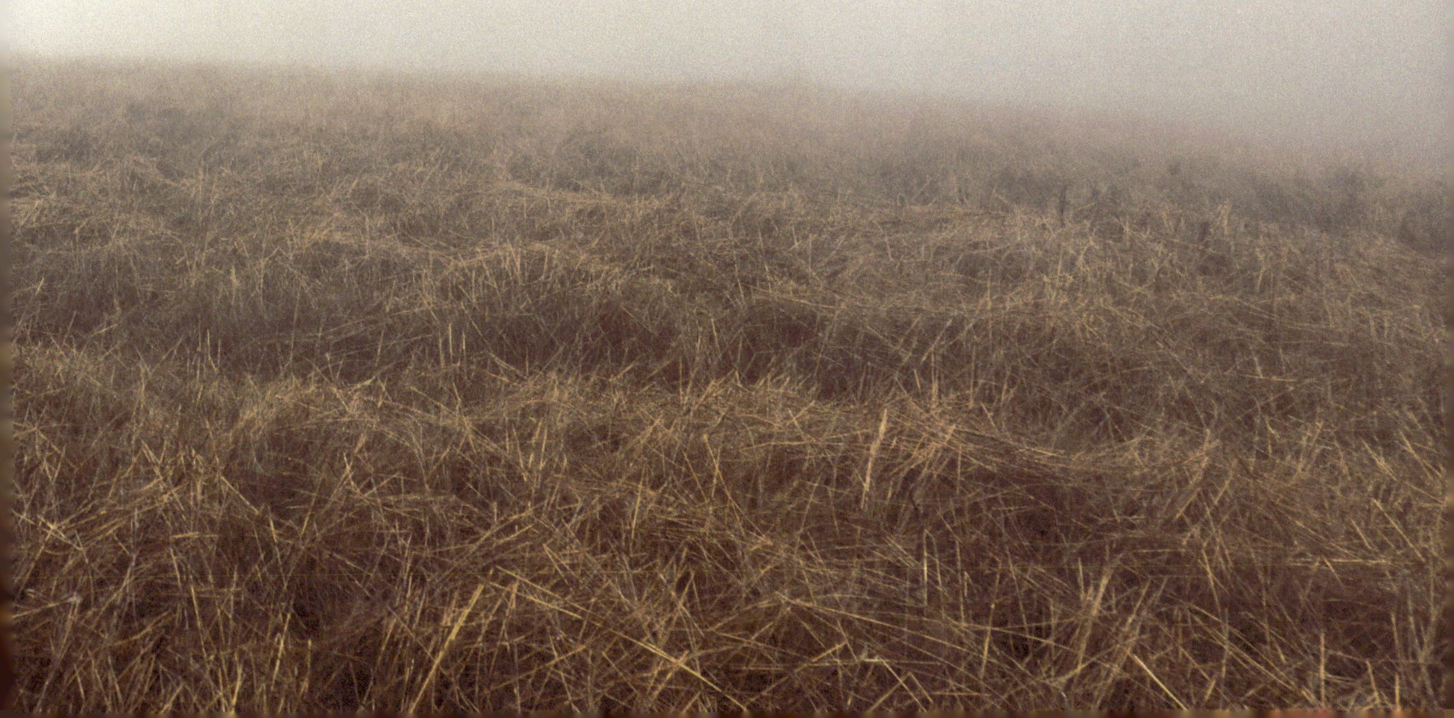

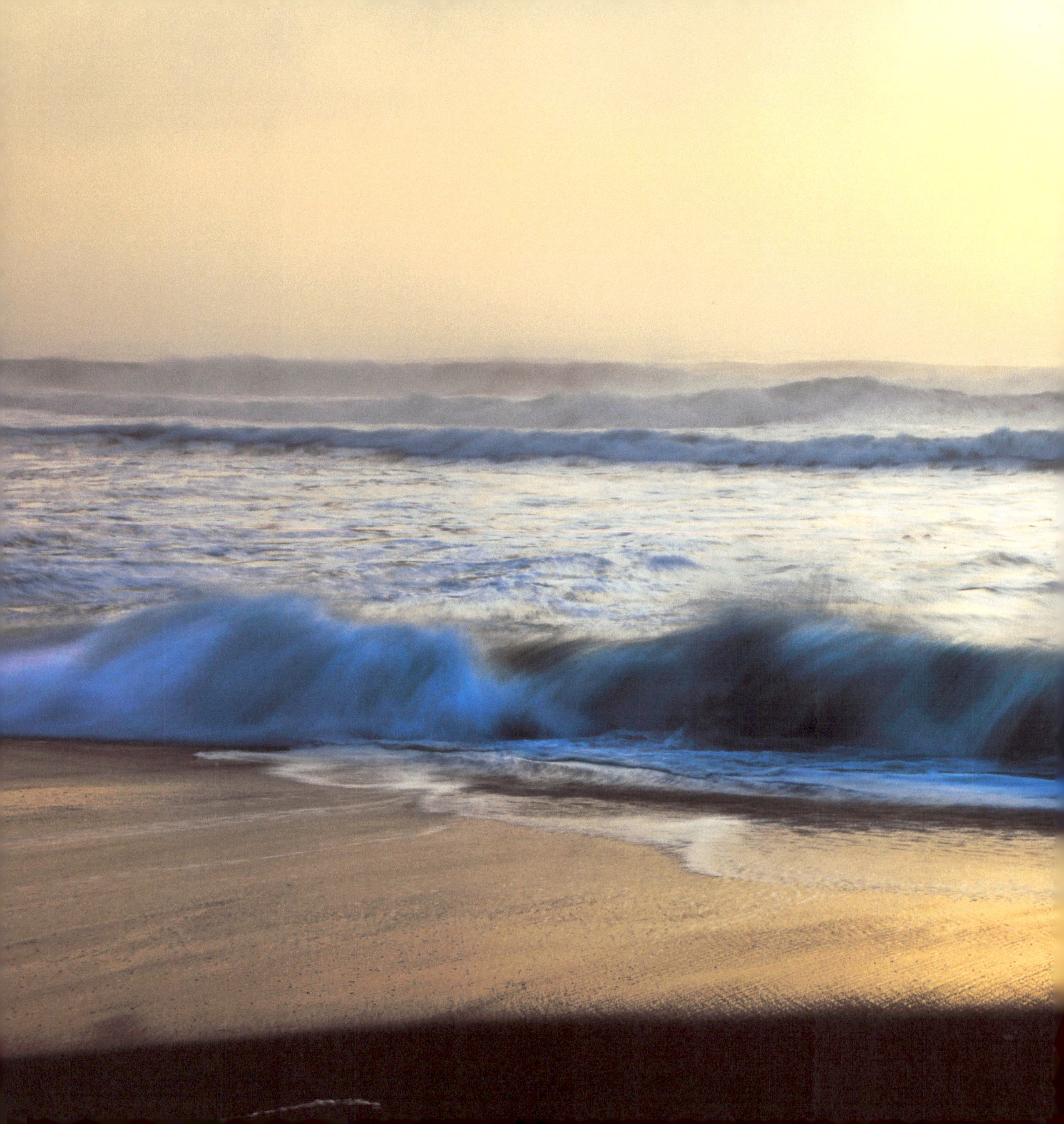

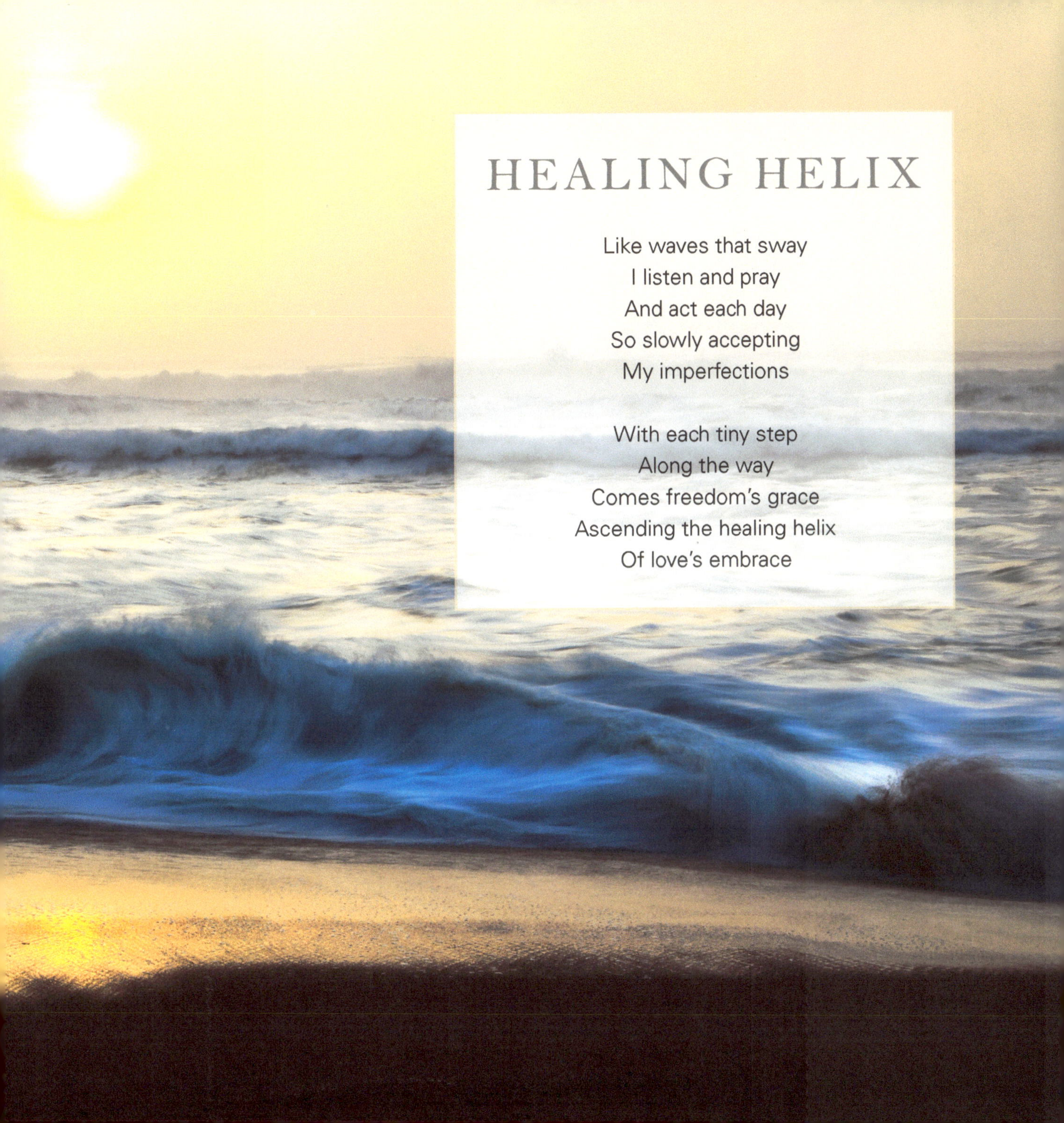

HEALING HELIX

Like waves that sway
I listen and pray
And act each day
So slowly accepting
My imperfections

With each tiny step
Along the way
Comes freedom's grace
Ascending the healing helix
Of love's embrace

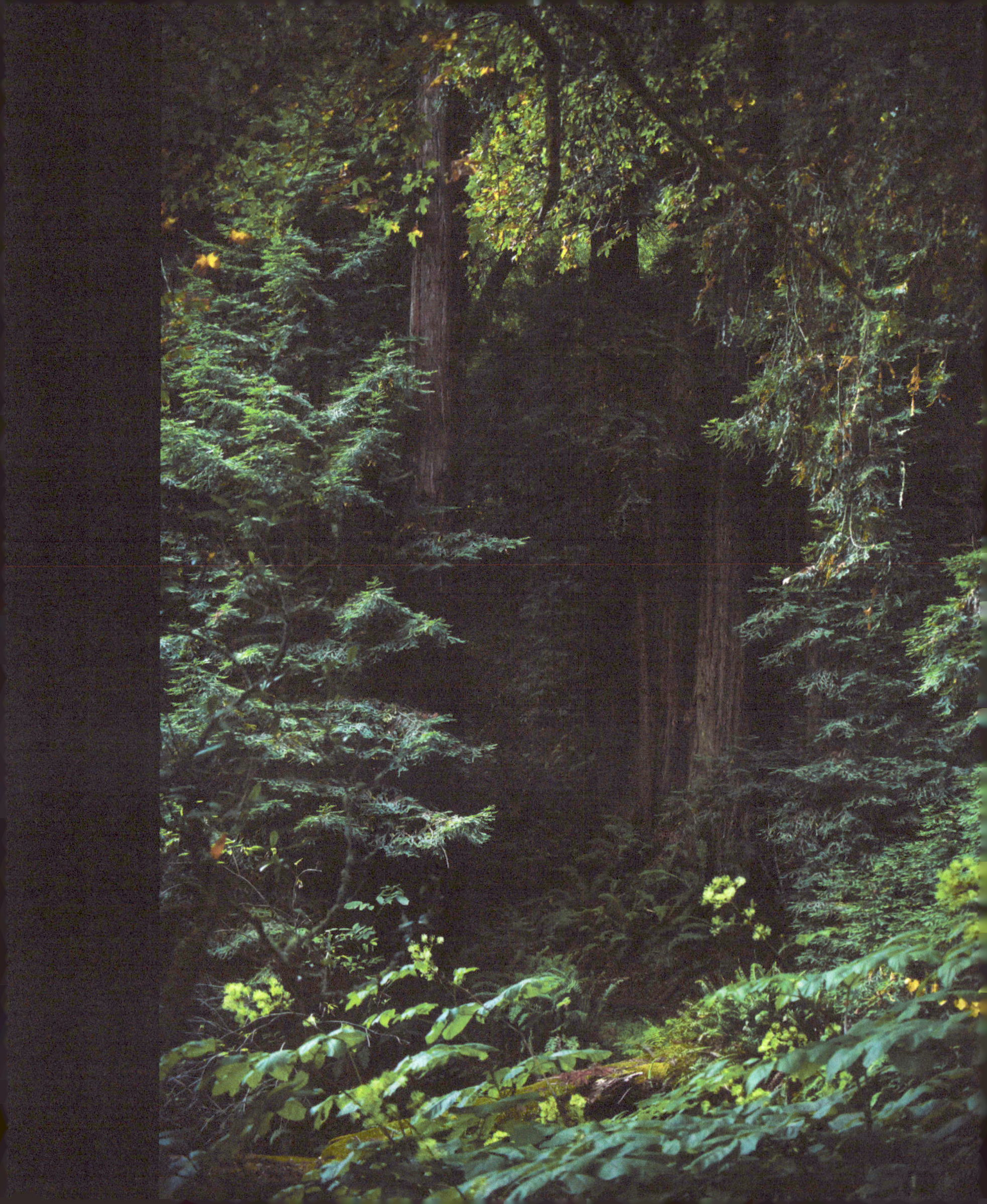

HOLD ME HERE

Hold me here
In this dark place
Hold my fears
In your embrace

My chest is hollow
My hands are cold
Your touch will sense
My soul unfold

My lonely eyes
Betray my face
Hold me here
In this dark place

And sucks the light
Into the blackest hole

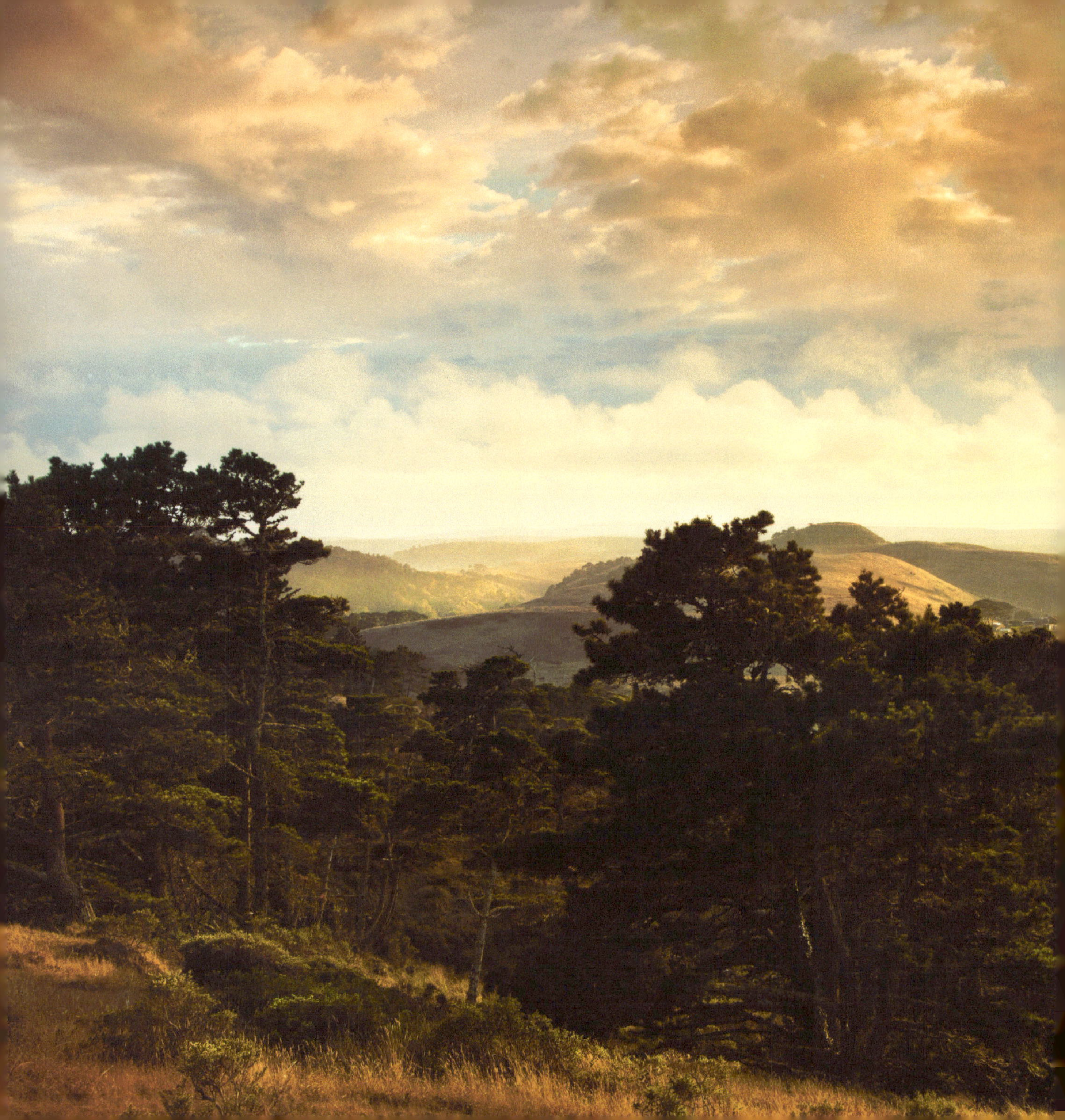

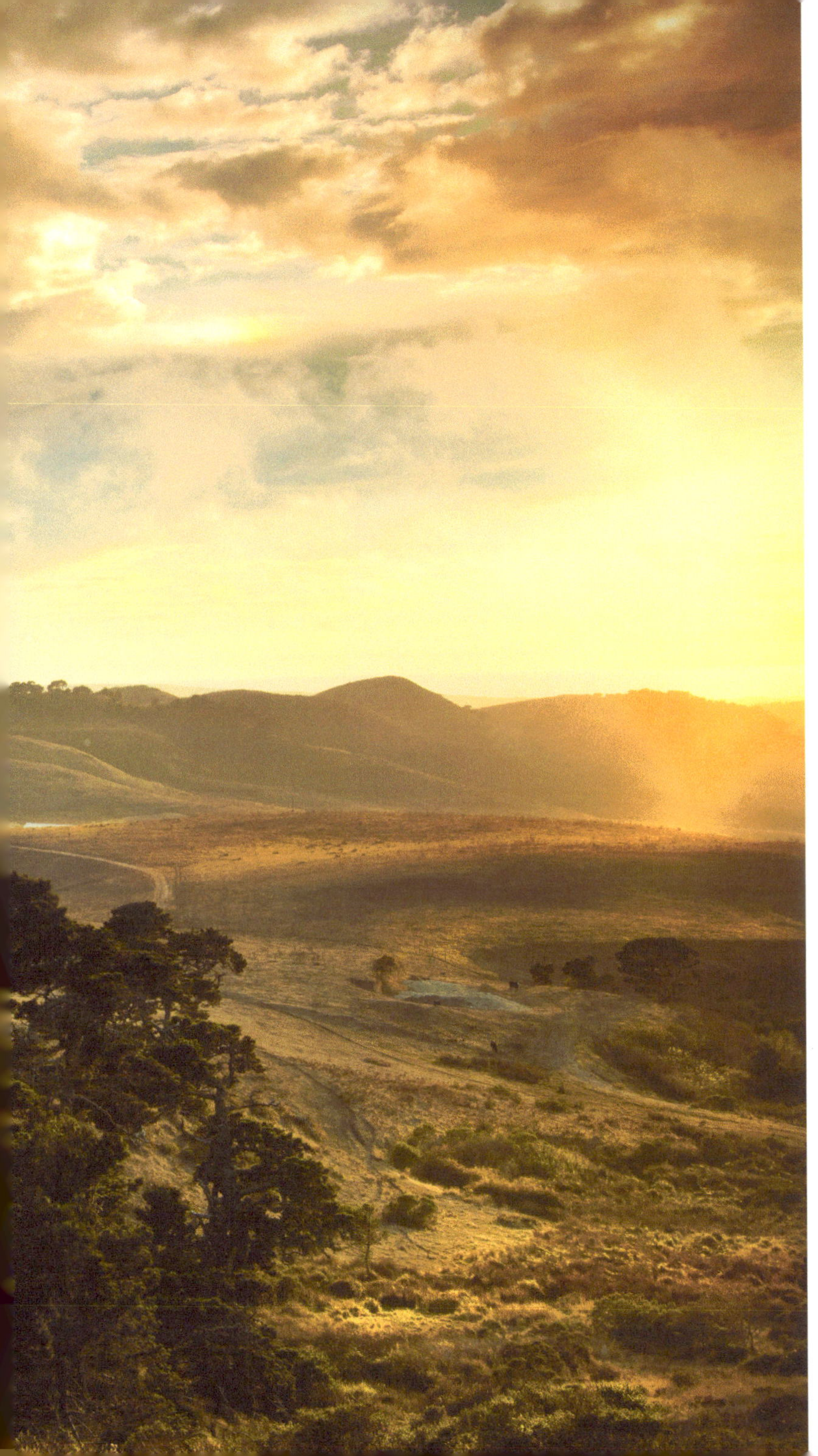

ENTER HERE

Deep in my listening heart
My beloved sings
A song of hope

The chorus churns
Constant fears
Disturbing waves
Stormy seas

But you, you're always there
Patiently waiting
Arms welcoming
My bridge

The calm comes
And begs me
Enter here

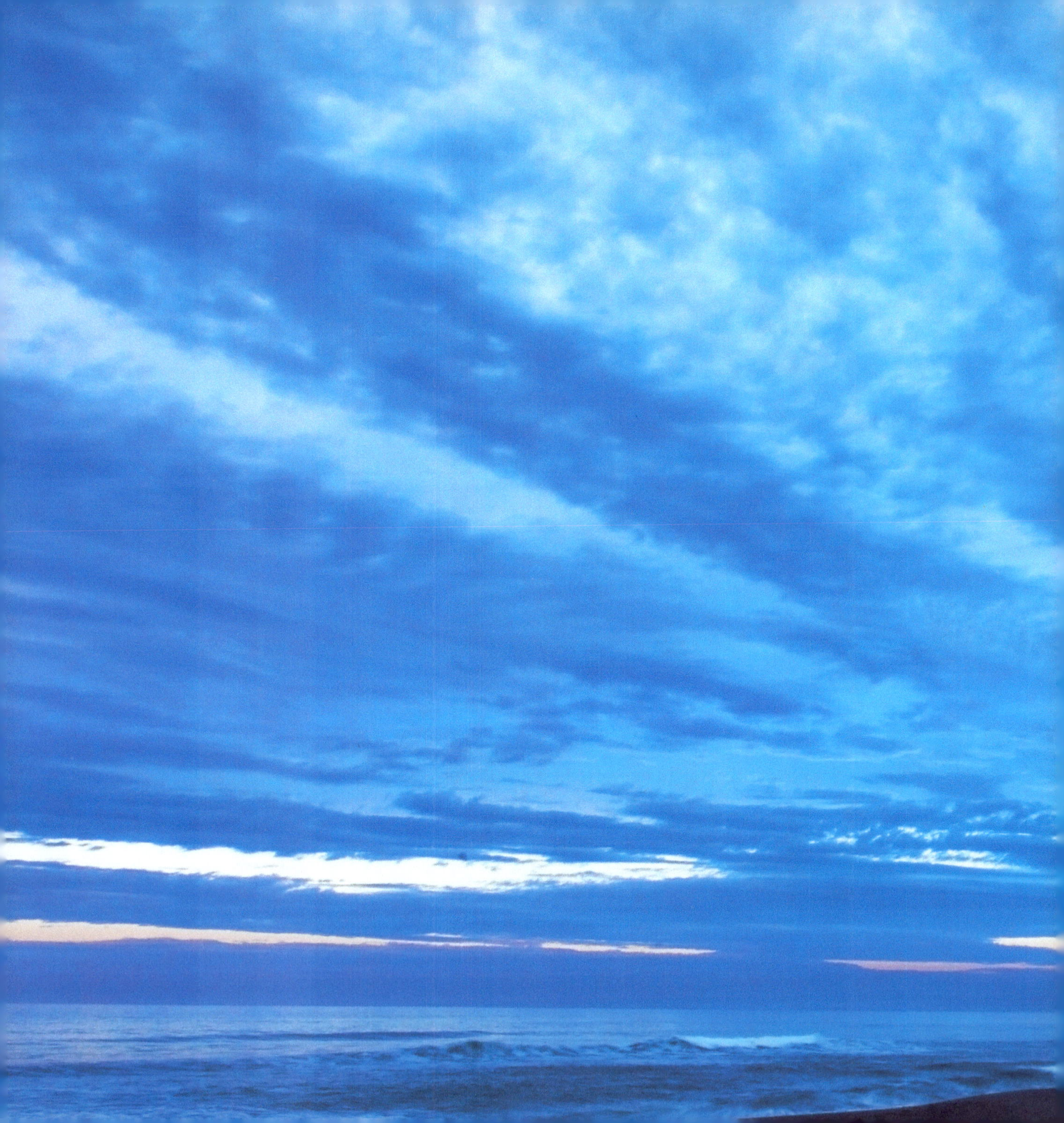

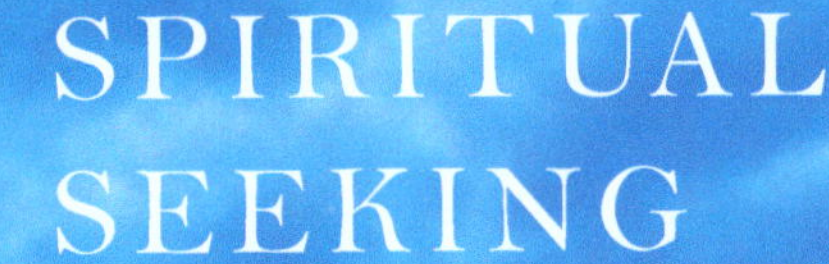

SPIRITUAL SEEKING

Spiritual seeking
Can fry your brain
You shouldn't suffer
But you feel the pain

Surrender ego
Don't hold back
Sit with the silence
Tough nut to crack

Live in the present
Don't rue the past
Don't fear the future
Hey, life is a blast

You're not your thoughts
The story's fake
Sometimes this path
Is tough to take

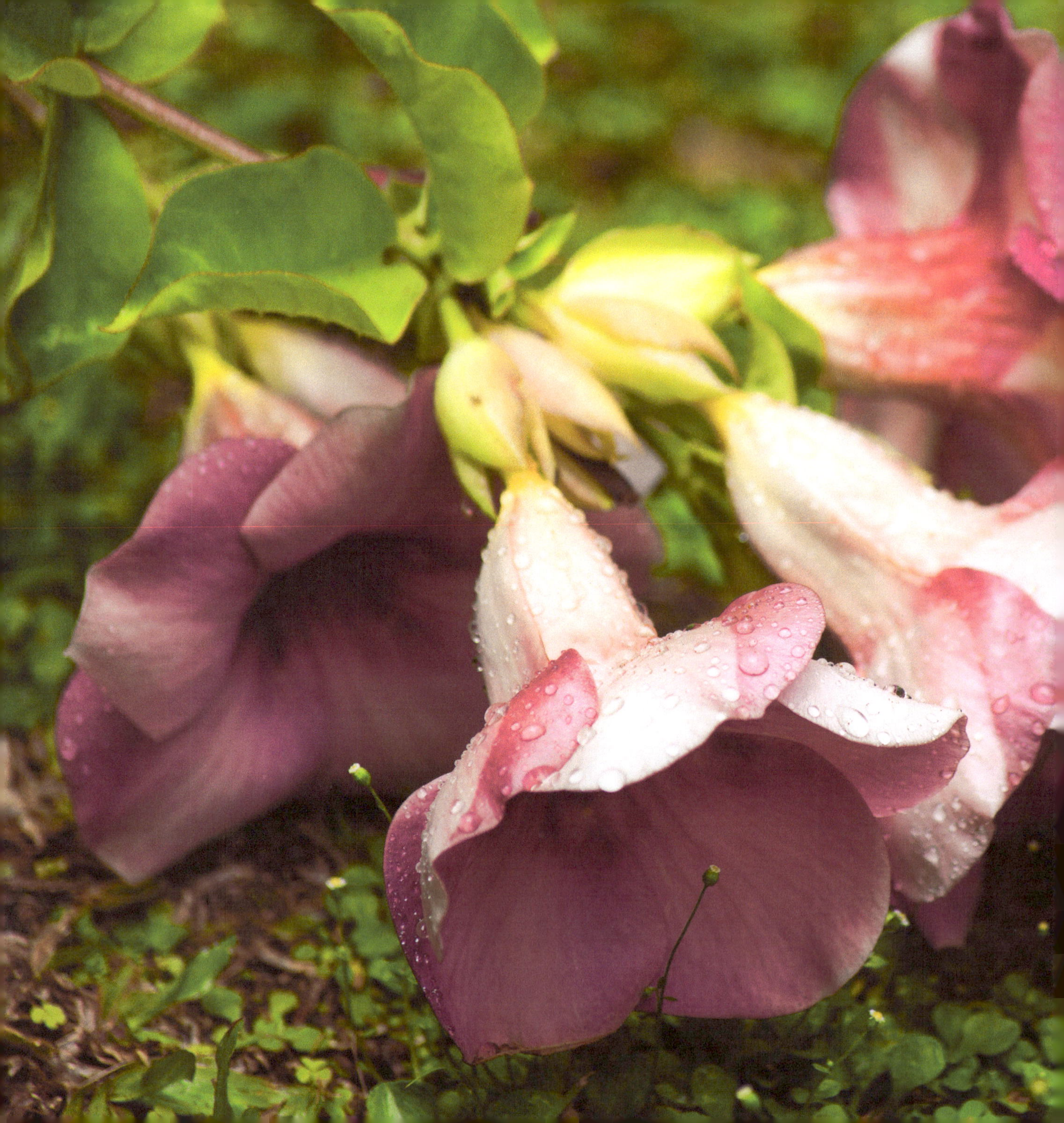

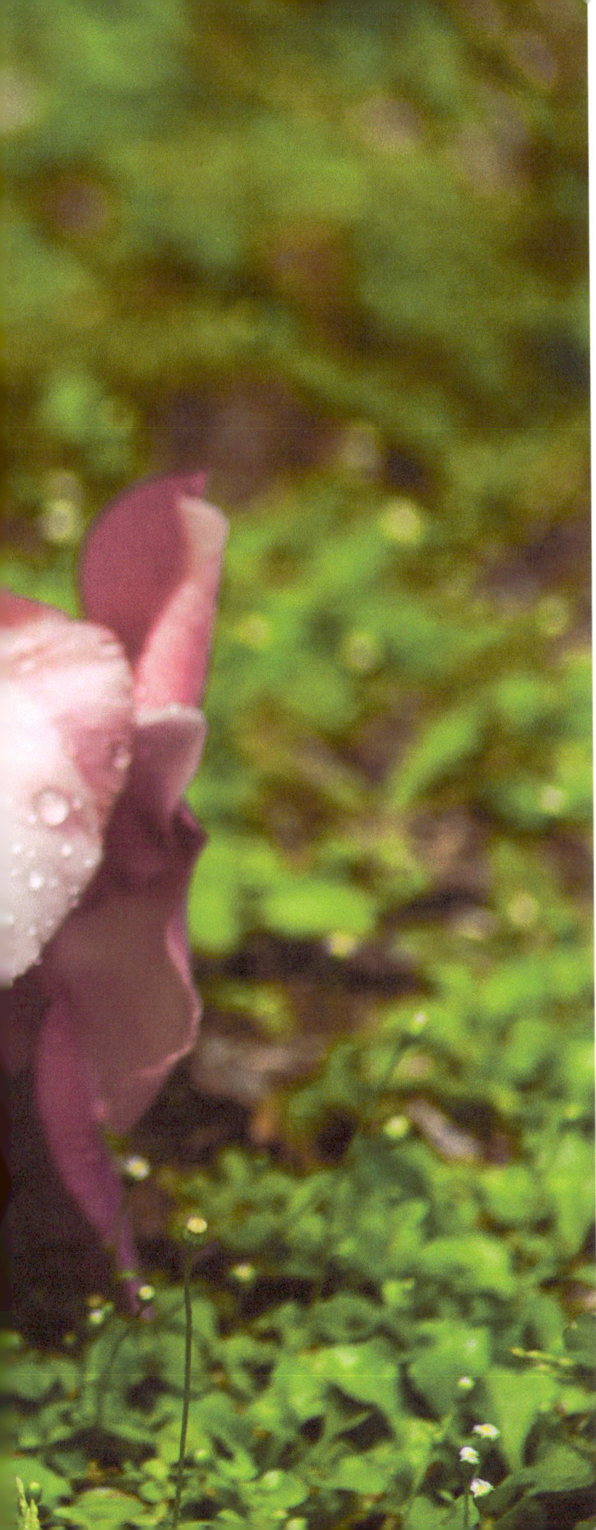

RICH SOIL

To plant a seed we rush sometimes
But soil must be rich
Our ancestors listened
To the moon and stars
To divine that time

Takes rich soil
For roots to take
For seeds to sprout

Takes patience to lay fallow
Like savasana, palms up
Eyes closed
Waiting for the rain

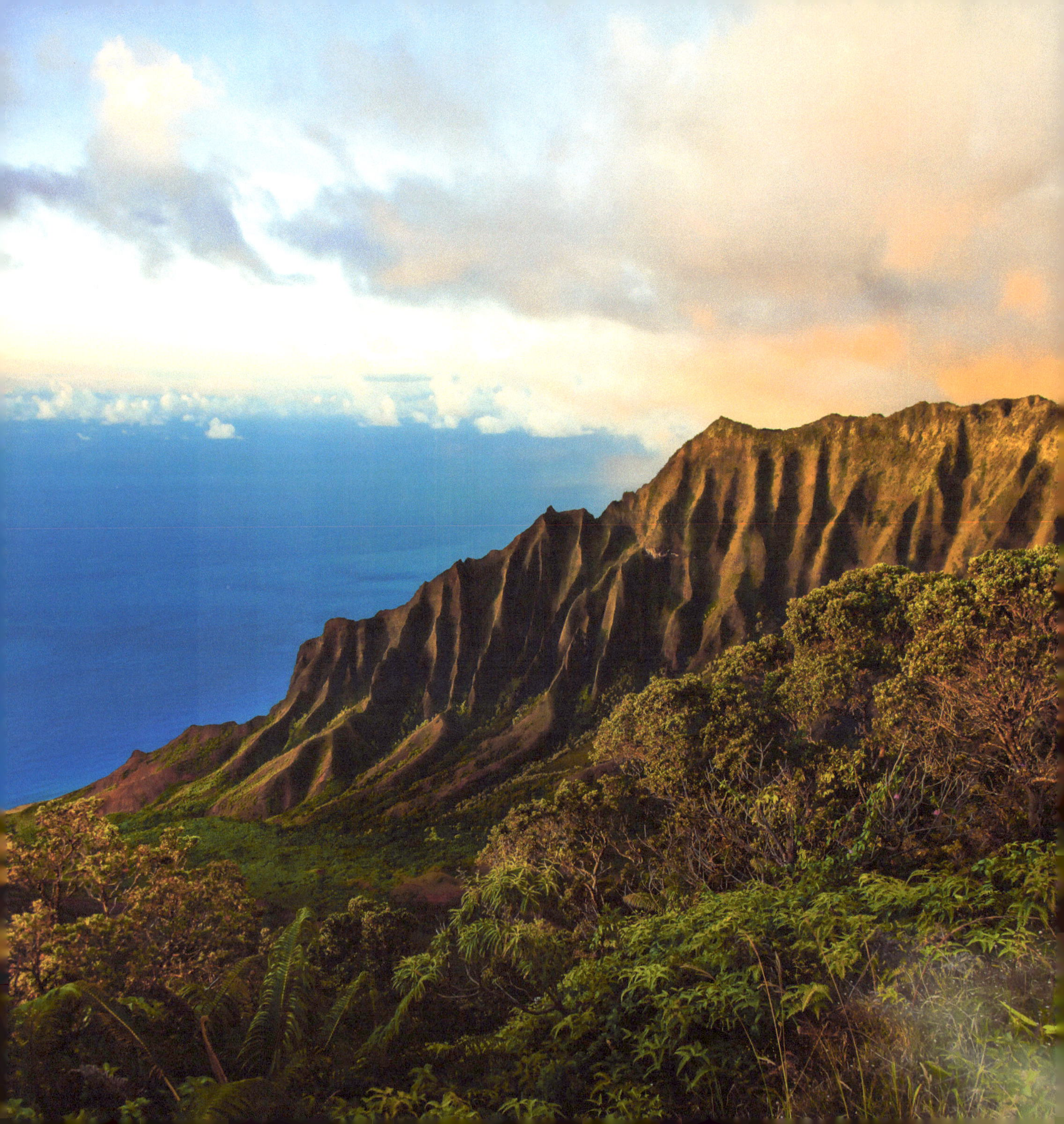

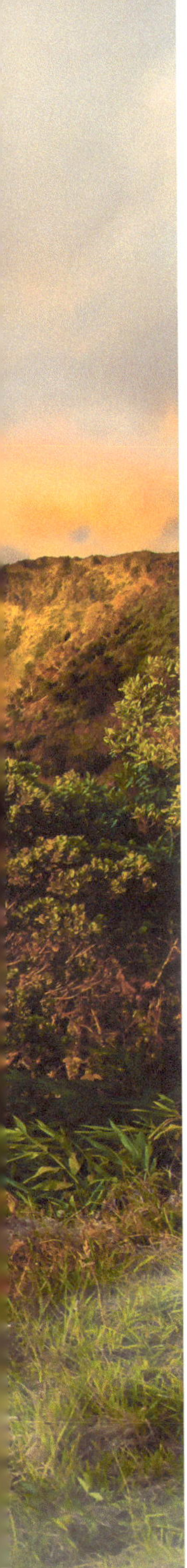

LONGING

Ferry me
To the morning mist
Float me
To the clouds
Fly me
Way above the sea
To live my life
Out loud

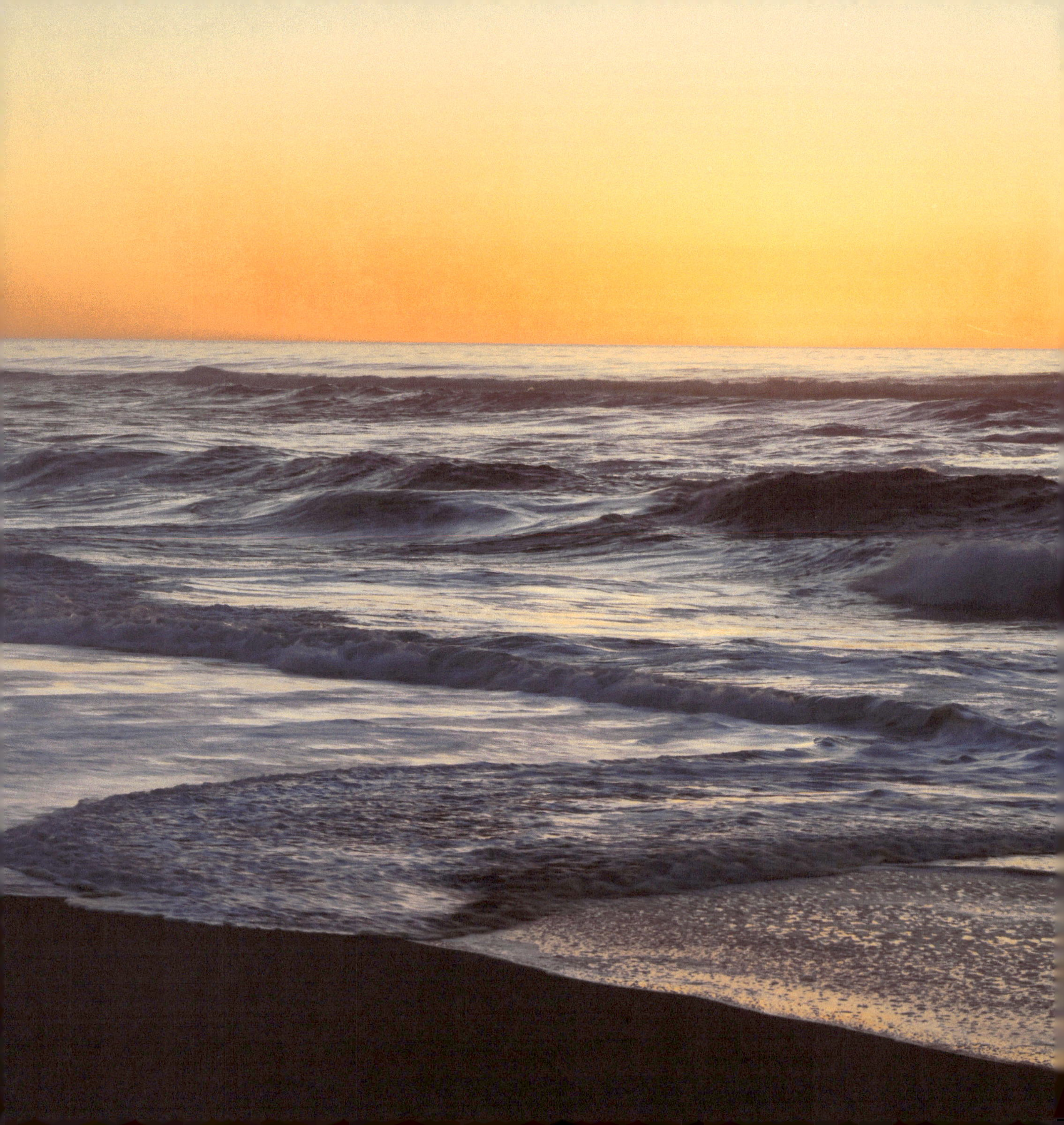

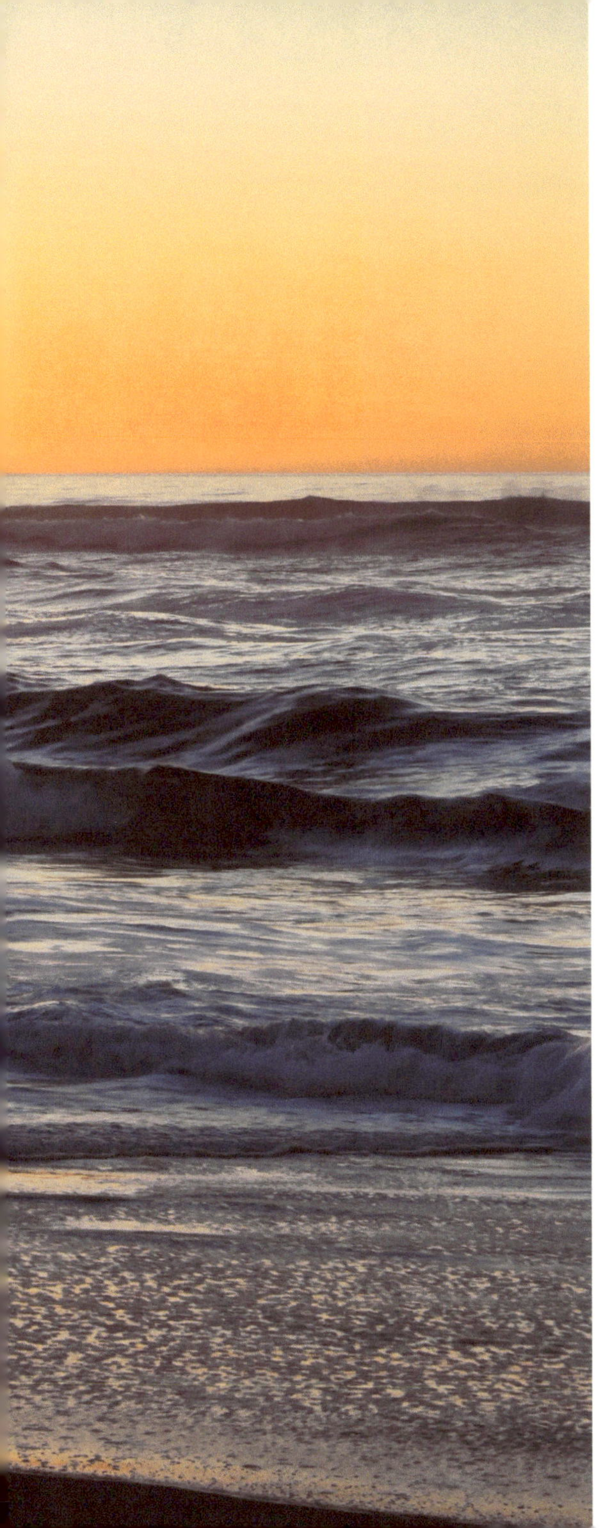

ADRIFT

I am so lonely
Adrift
Rocking and roiling
In deep, dark waters
Allowing waves
Of careless thought
To take me
Where
I need not go

Where are you, sunrise?
Where is your rising glory?
I miss the glow that
Held me
Unplugged my mind
Enflamed my heart

Now here I lay
In stillness
On the beach
A living corpse
Waves washing up over my body
Between my toes and fingers
I hear wind chimes floating by
Tubular tones
Softly calling me
Softly calling me
I close my eyes and see

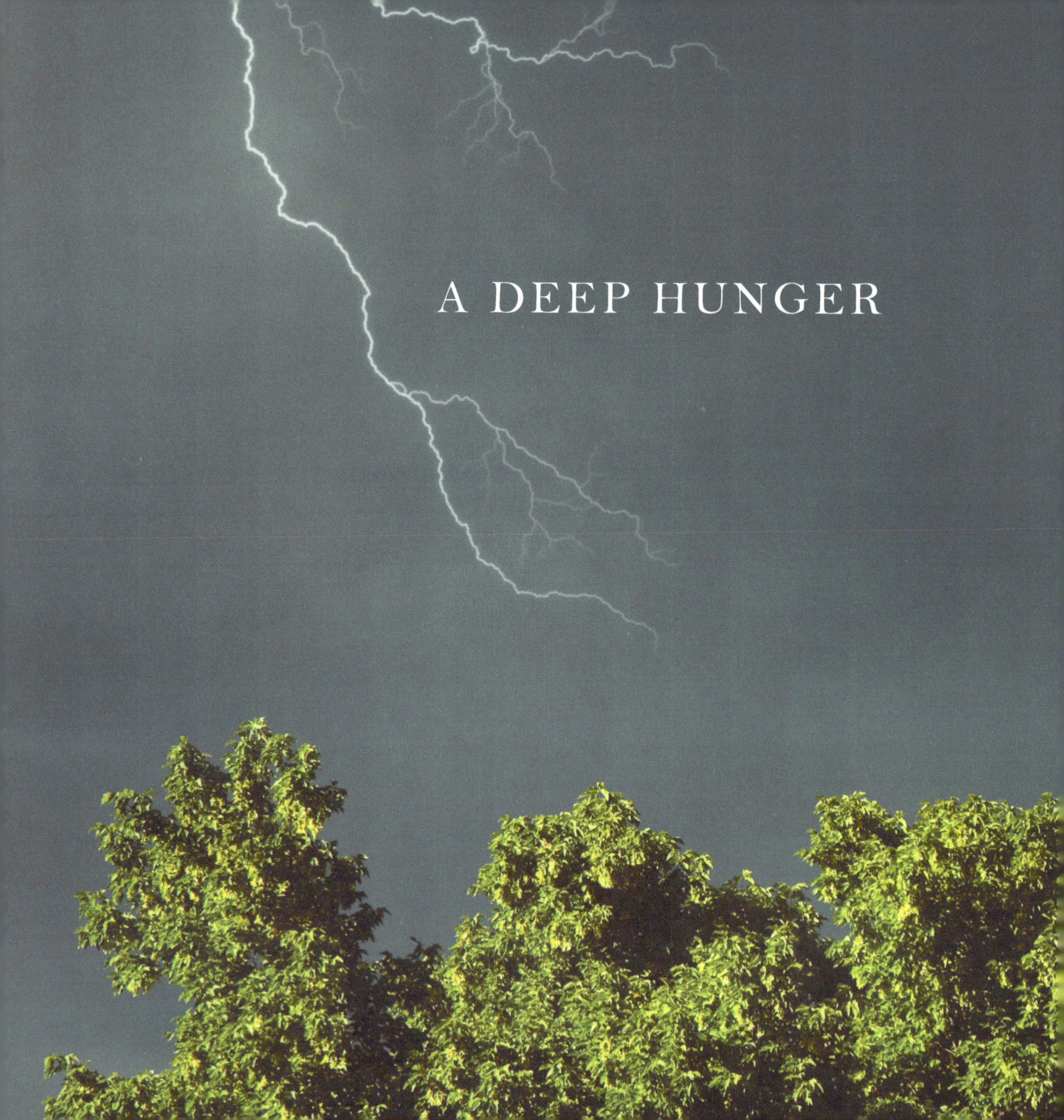

A DEEP HUNGER

I hear distant rumblings
Rolling in
As lightning slaps
The darkness

A deep hunger
Calls my name
Deep, deep hunger
But I turn away

My heart wants
Refuge
It aches
In silence
Lost and lonely

Then I hear
A murmur
A whisper
The swift sense
Of a visitor
A protector

May I rest here
Unclench my jaw
My thighs
My eyes
My soul

Unclench my soul
I pray on my knees
Open my heart
Let out
The pain
Let in
The love
That love that waits
Like the wind
Like heaven
Unseen but felt

Take my will
Take it!

The weight of my will
Crushes hope
Distorts time
Suffocates love

Take it please

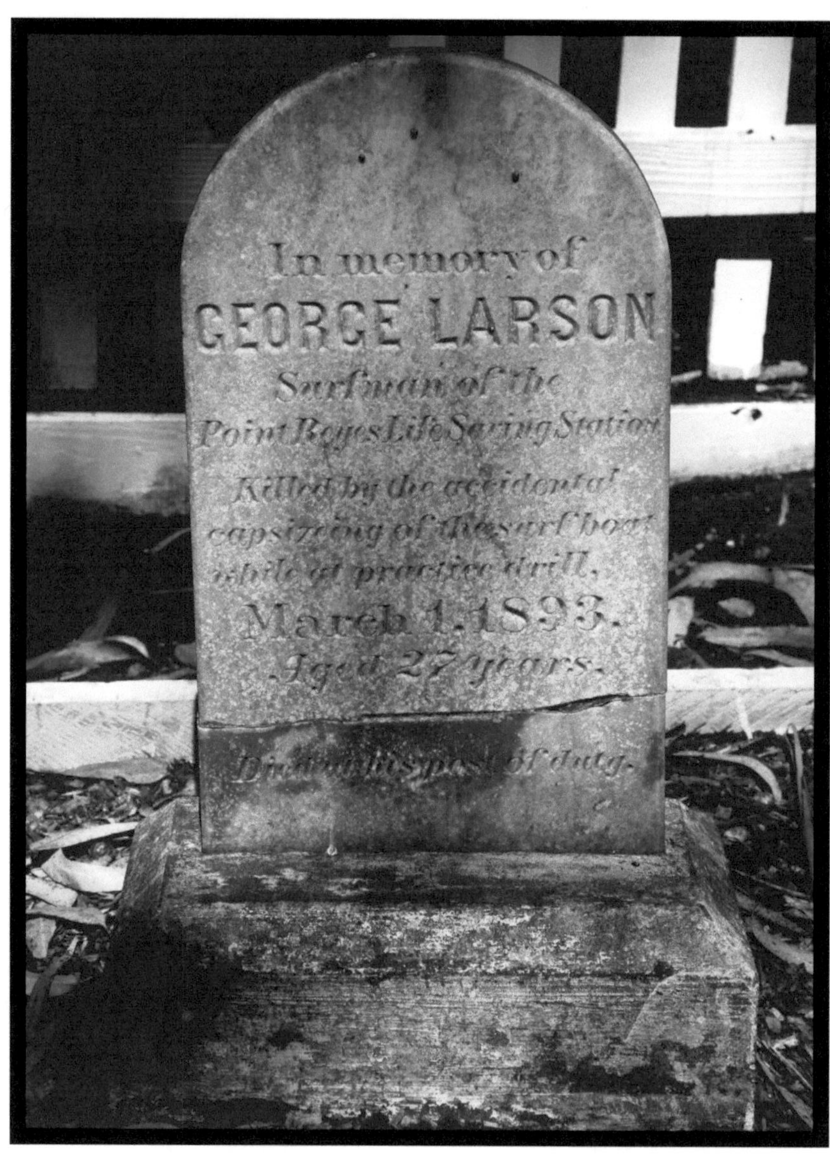
In memory of
GEORGE LARSON
Surfman of the
Point Reyes Life Saving Station
Killed by the accidental
capsizing of the surf boat
while at practice drill,
March 1. 1893.
Aged 27 years.

YOU'RE GONNA DIE

I'm sorry to tell you
That you're gonna die
It's not a 'what if?'
It's a when

We all have an hour
We know not which one
If we knew it for certain
What then?

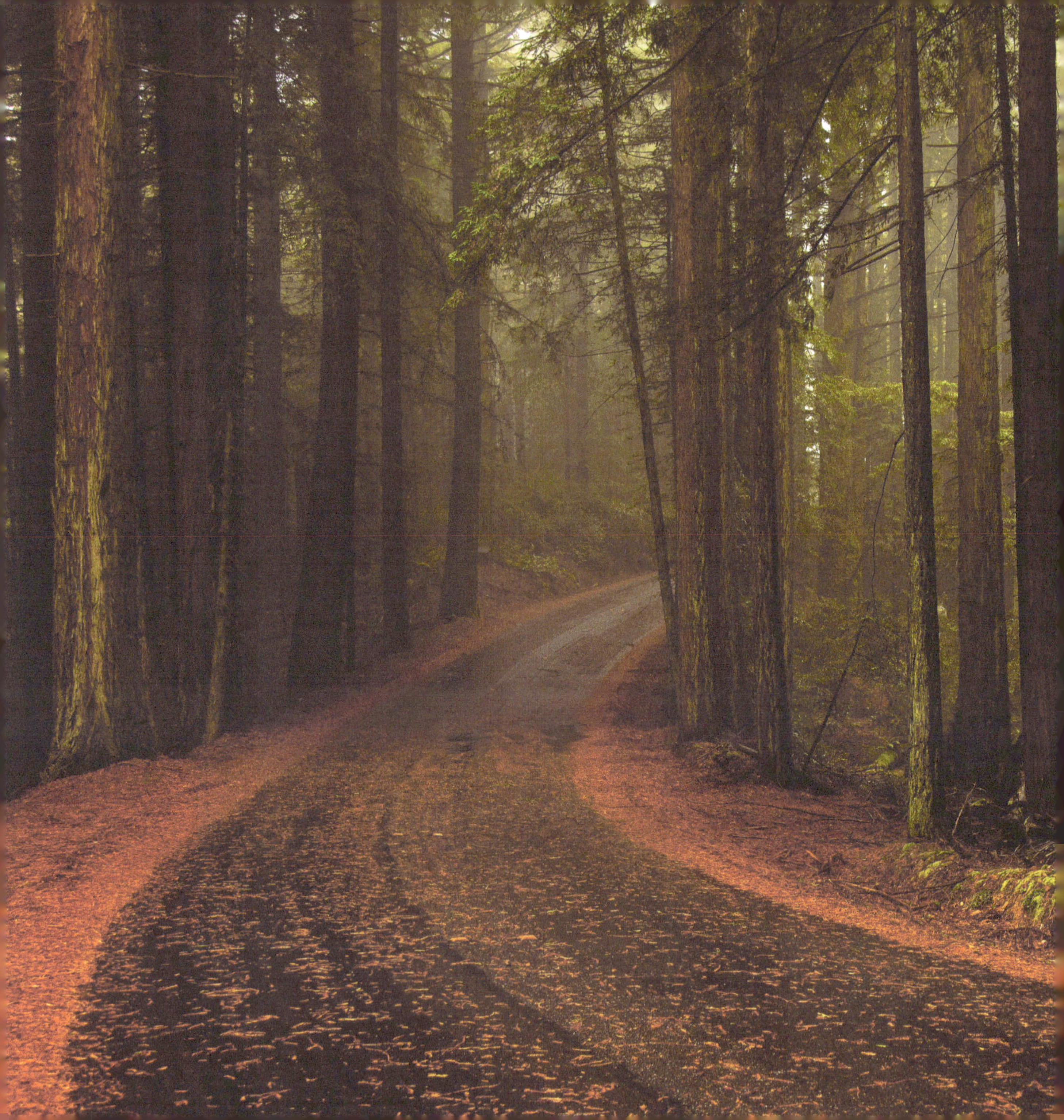

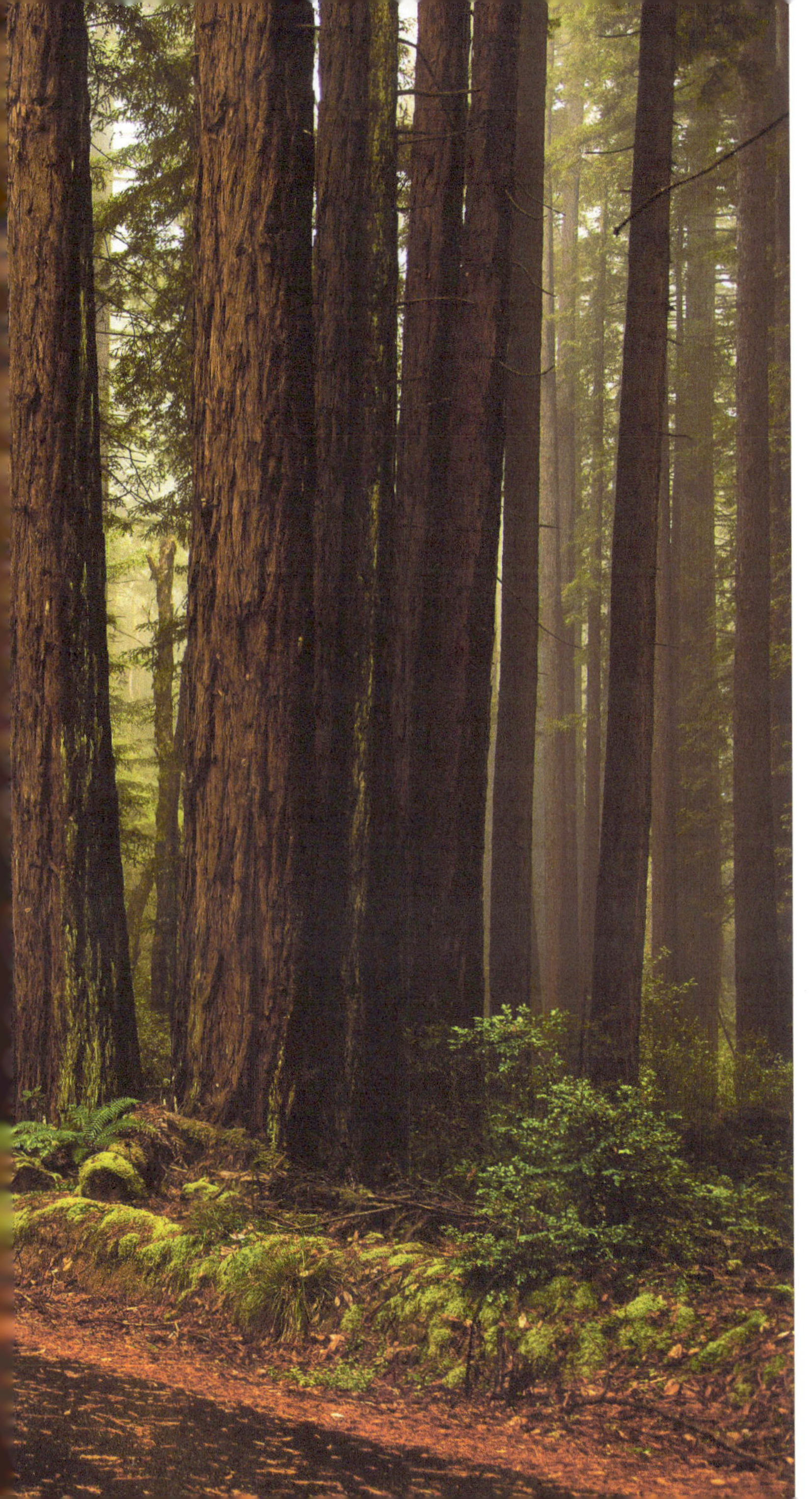

FORGIVENESS

Do you leap
Or slip
Into forgiveness?

Does the mournful dove
Sound her call
For me?

Does the earth wait in silence
Or tremble with love?

Now I hear
Celestial symphonies
Soaring with joy!

Whirling angels
Call me
Along the winding path

Call me
By name

Call me
Into love's
Most patient arms

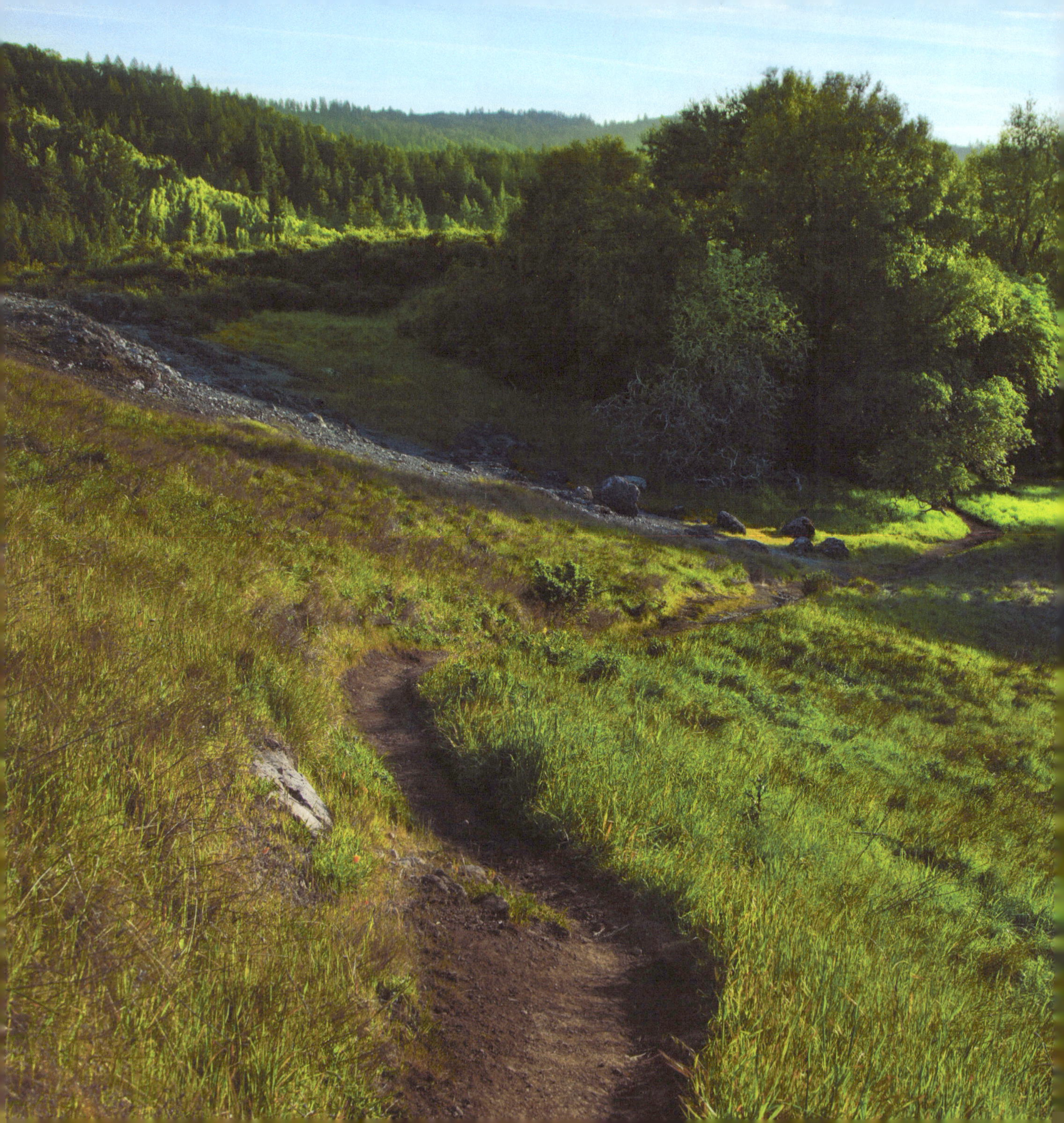

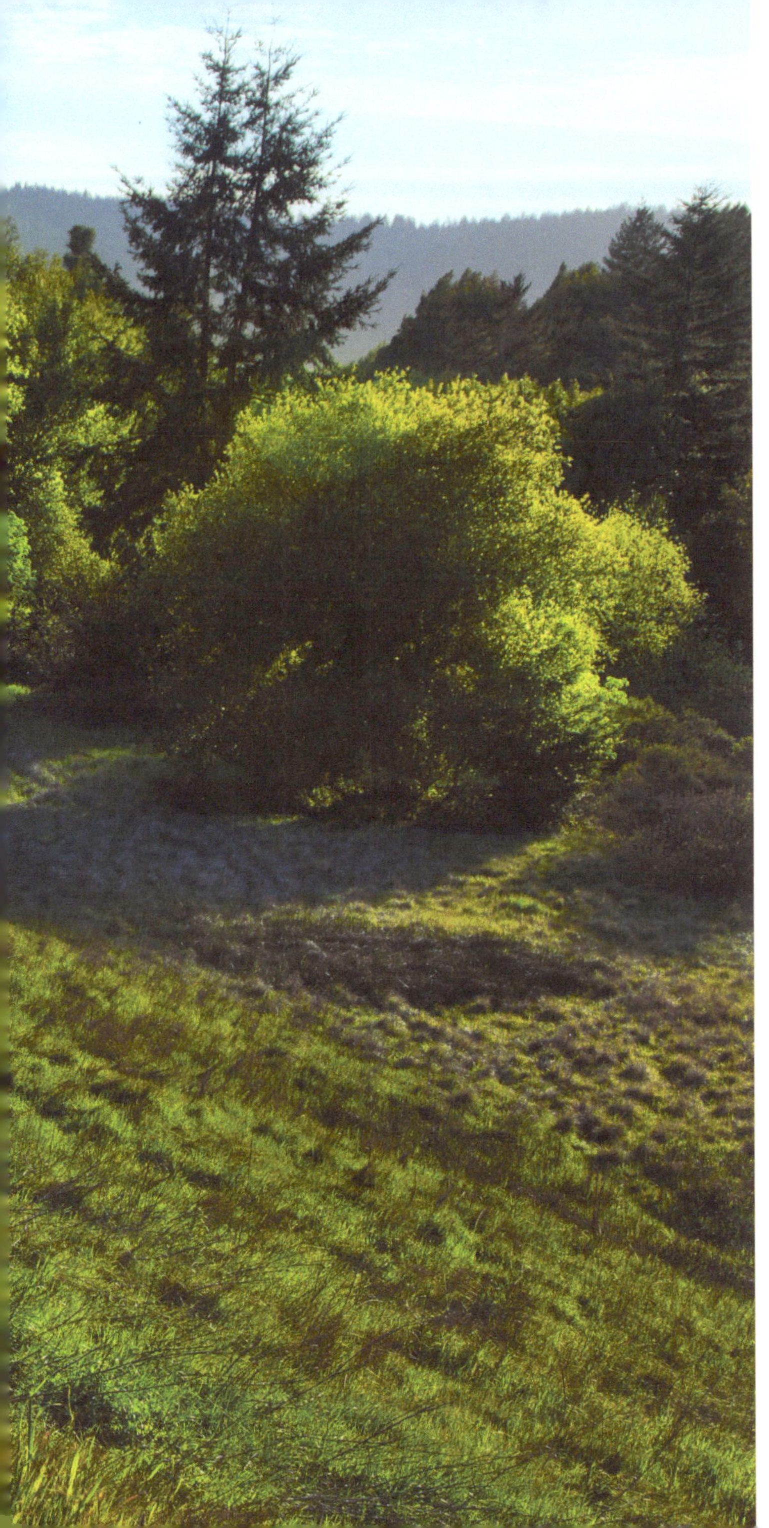

IN THIS STILLNESS

Everything
All the answers
All the questions
Lie waiting
In this stillness

The mirage of
A busy life
Distracts from
The beauty
Of the desert

The quiet
Settles my heart
The light
Lifts my spirit
I listen
For your love

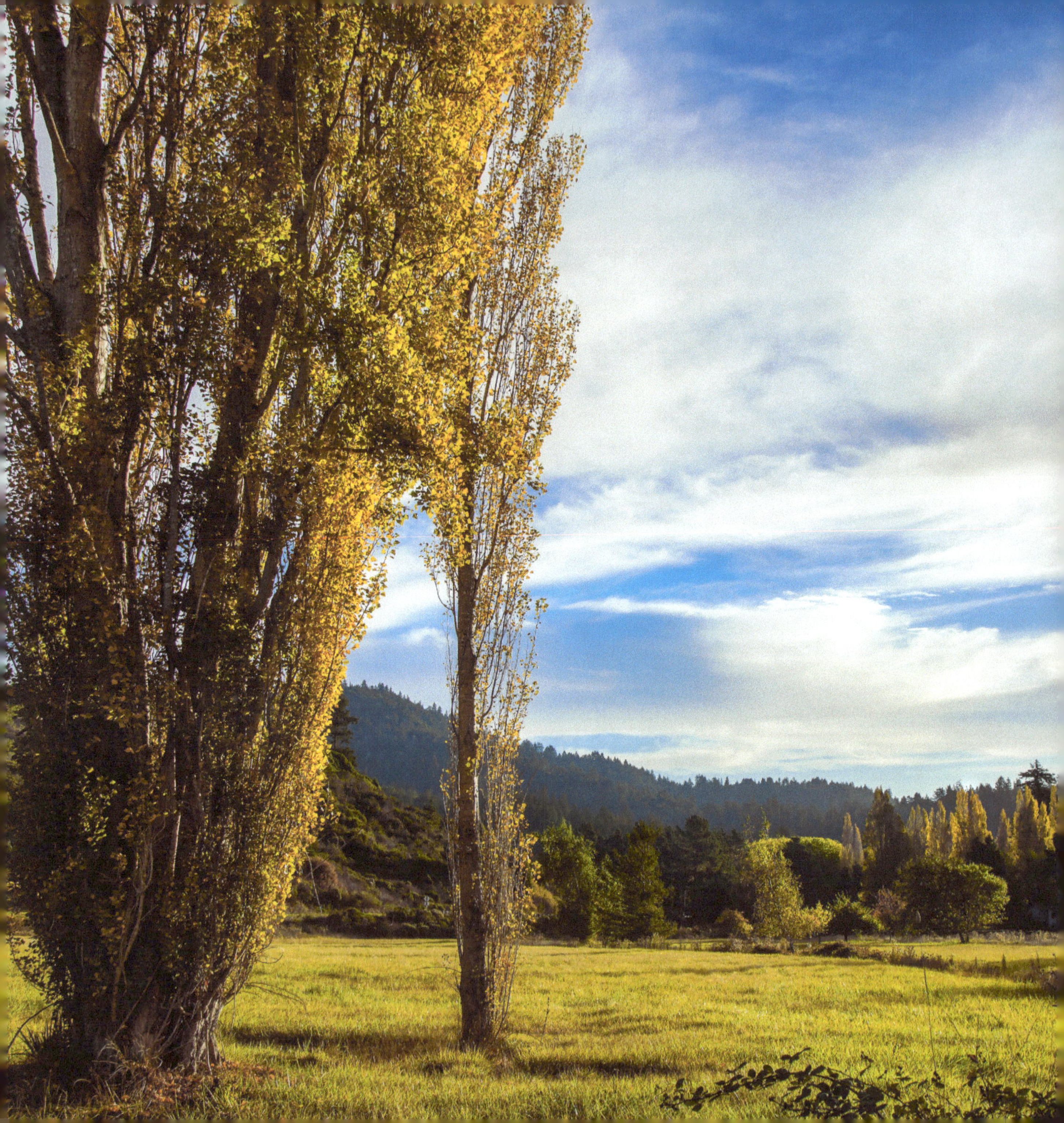

IT'S ALWAYS ABOUT LOVE

It's always about love
Isn't it?
The weary weight
You bear on your shoulders
With every step
Every day

It's always about love
The kind you wall away
Until it tries to peek through
Say hello...
But you say
Go away
I can not bear your presence

It's always about love
The people pleasing
Approval seeking
Shopping
Eating
Drinking
More

When all we want is
A warm embrace
Someone to welcome us
At the door
Even a wagging tail
Can help

A question:
Can we set our dial
To 'receive'
Not with a tip of the cap
A curtsy
Not phony talk
Not phony listening

I mean
Can you receeeeive?
Drink it in deeply
Let it land
Right between your eyes
Without turning your head

Can you sit still
Feel what people feel
For you
For YOU?

Can you handle the truth
Of your goodness
It's what you
Want
Crave
Need

And after you have tried on
Every imaginable story
Cried yourself to sleep
Trudged through cold and dark
Clutched at false gods...

When you are ready
Finally
To admit you can't control
Your life
You can't

Then
And only then
You are ready
To enter the land
Where it's always about love

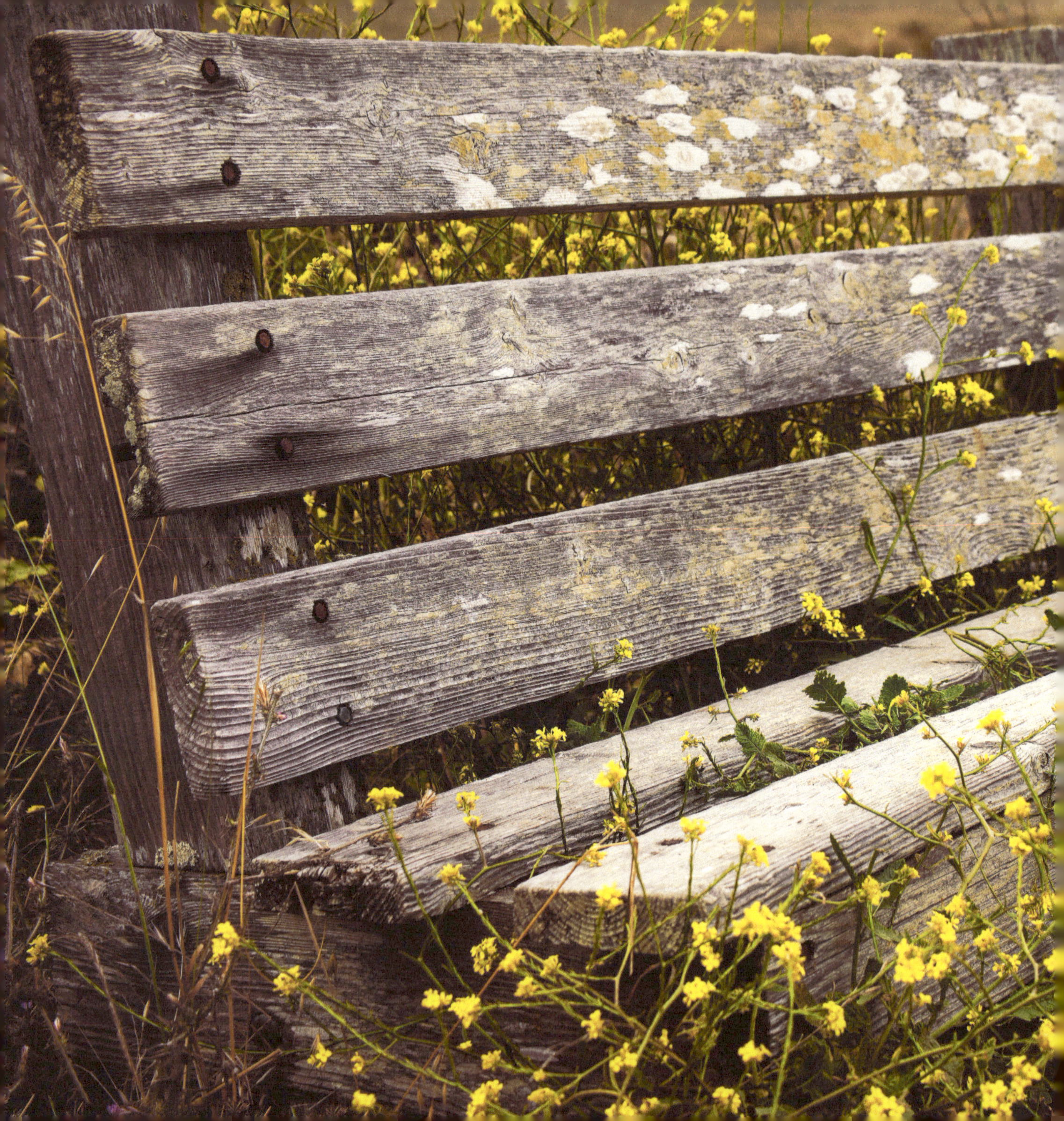

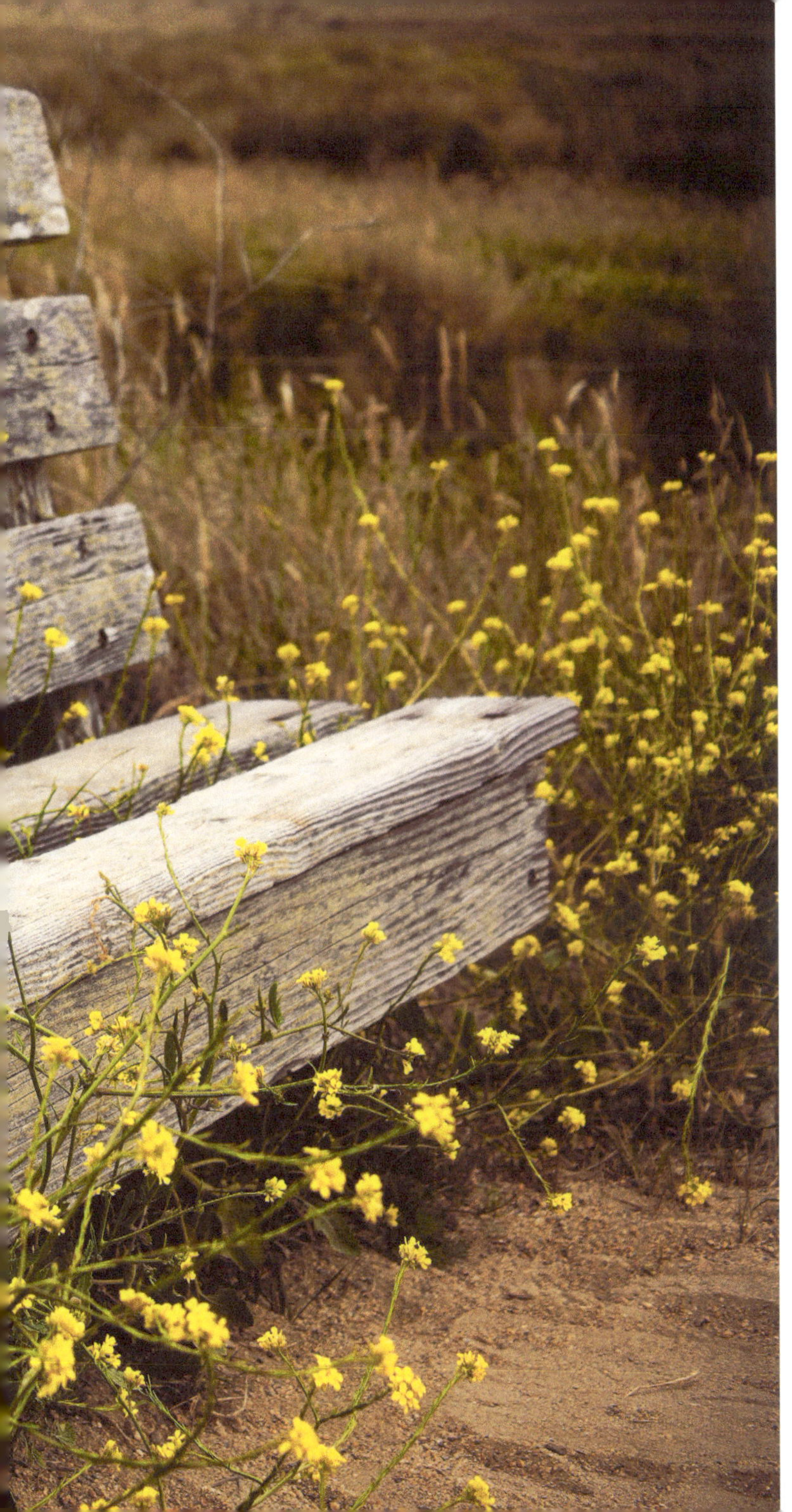

REST EASY

Rest easy
Touch my face
Transform yourself
Feel my embrace

Your head is heavy
Worn with worry
Slow your thoughts
Release the hurry

Take the fish
Not the snake
Feel the sun
Not the ache

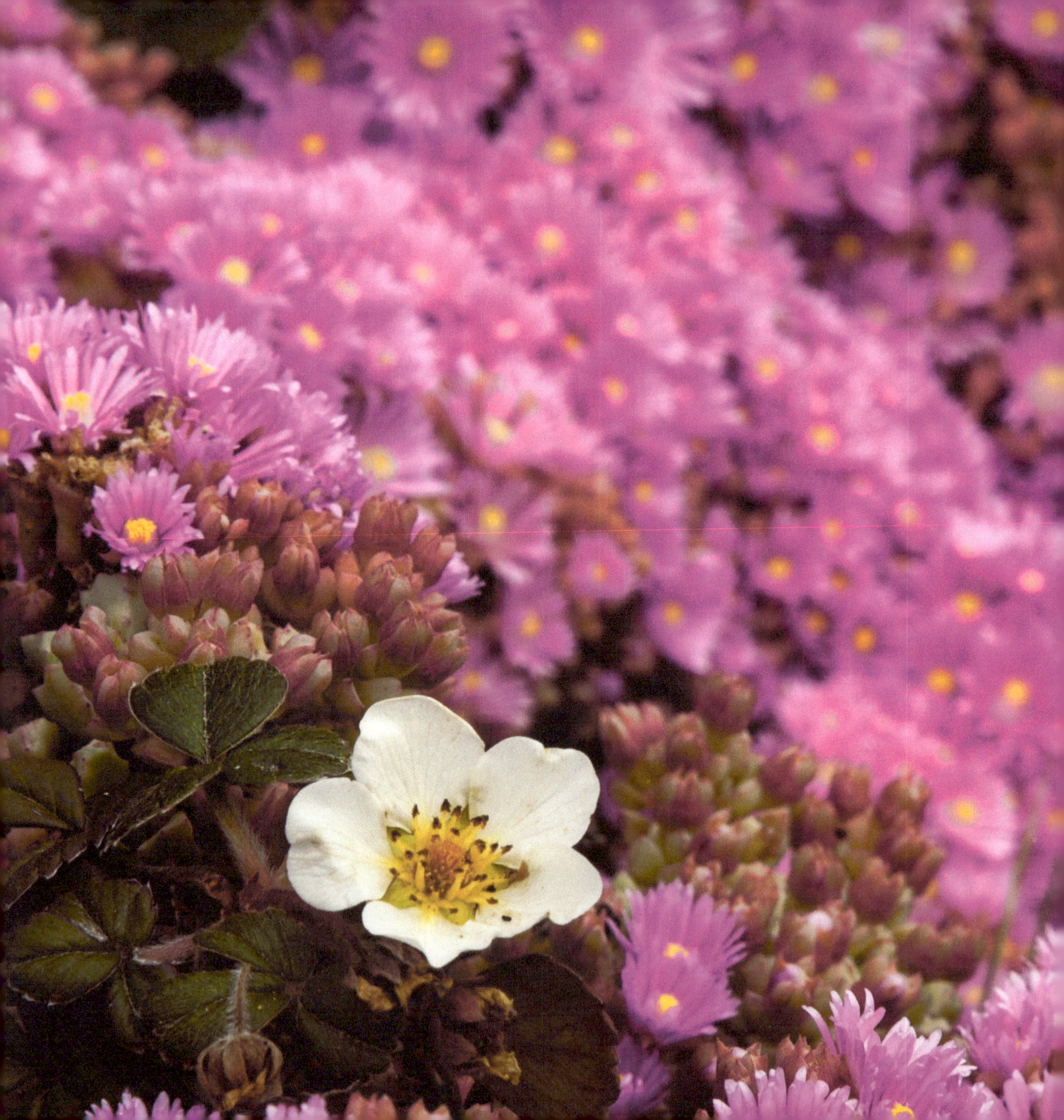

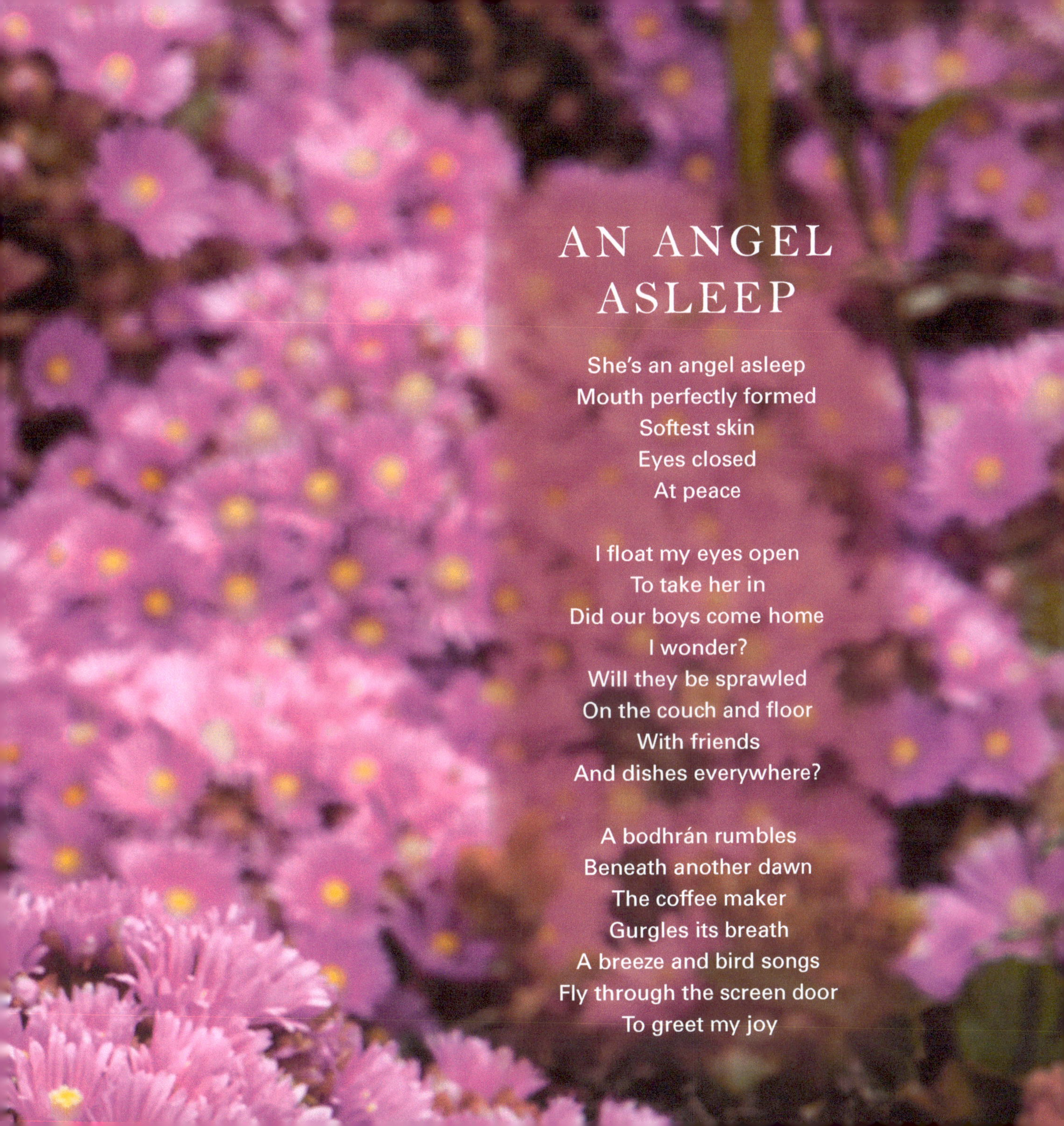

AN ANGEL ASLEEP

She's an angel asleep
Mouth perfectly formed
Softest skin
Eyes closed
At peace

I float my eyes open
To take her in
Did our boys come home
I wonder?
Will they be sprawled
On the couch and floor
With friends
And dishes everywhere?

A bodhrán rumbles
Beneath another dawn
The coffee maker
Gurgles its breath
A breeze and bird songs
Fly through the screen door
To greet my joy

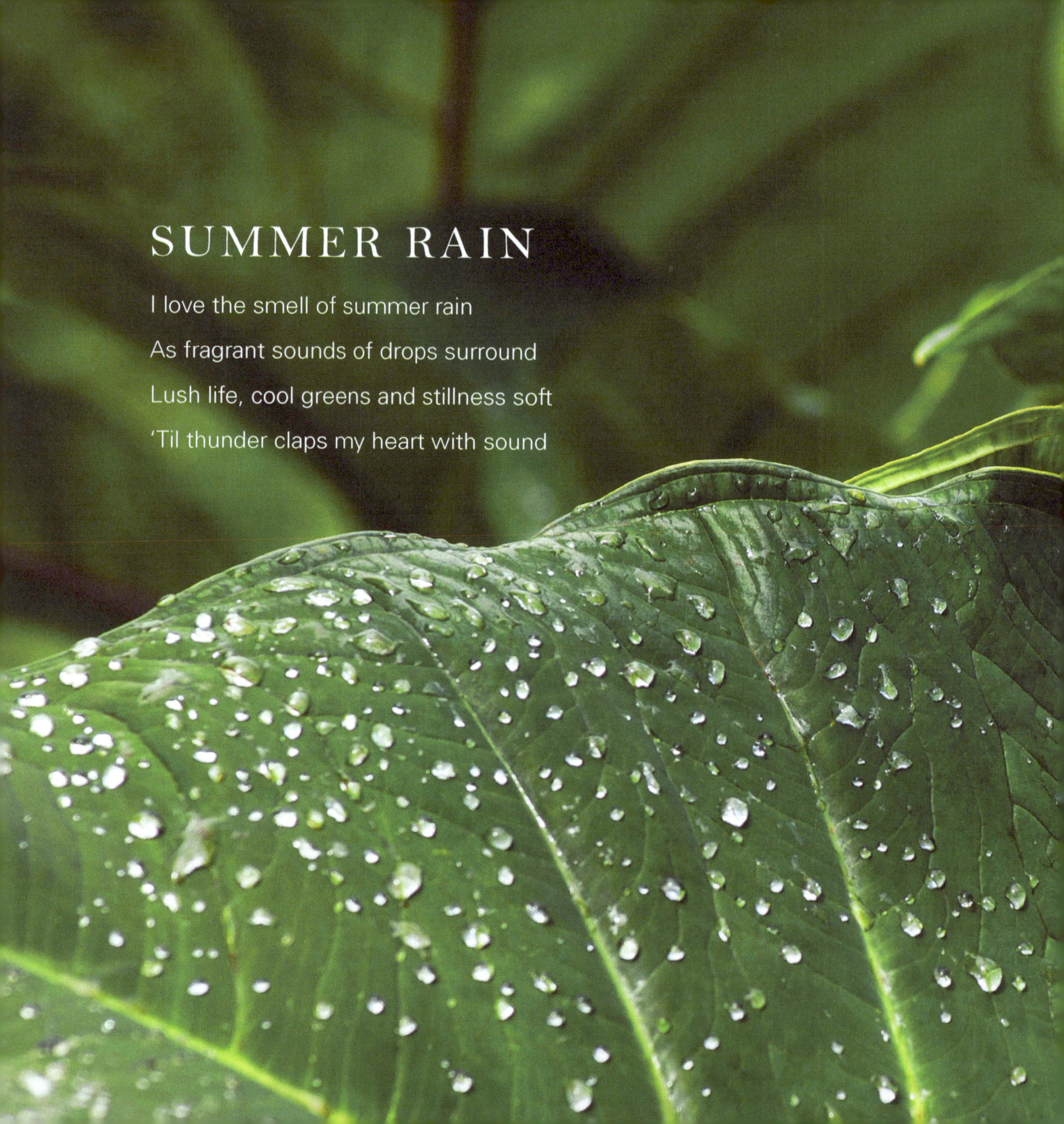

SUMMER RAIN

I love the smell of summer rain
As fragrant sounds of drops surround
Lush life, cool greens and stillness soft
'Til thunder claps my heart with sound

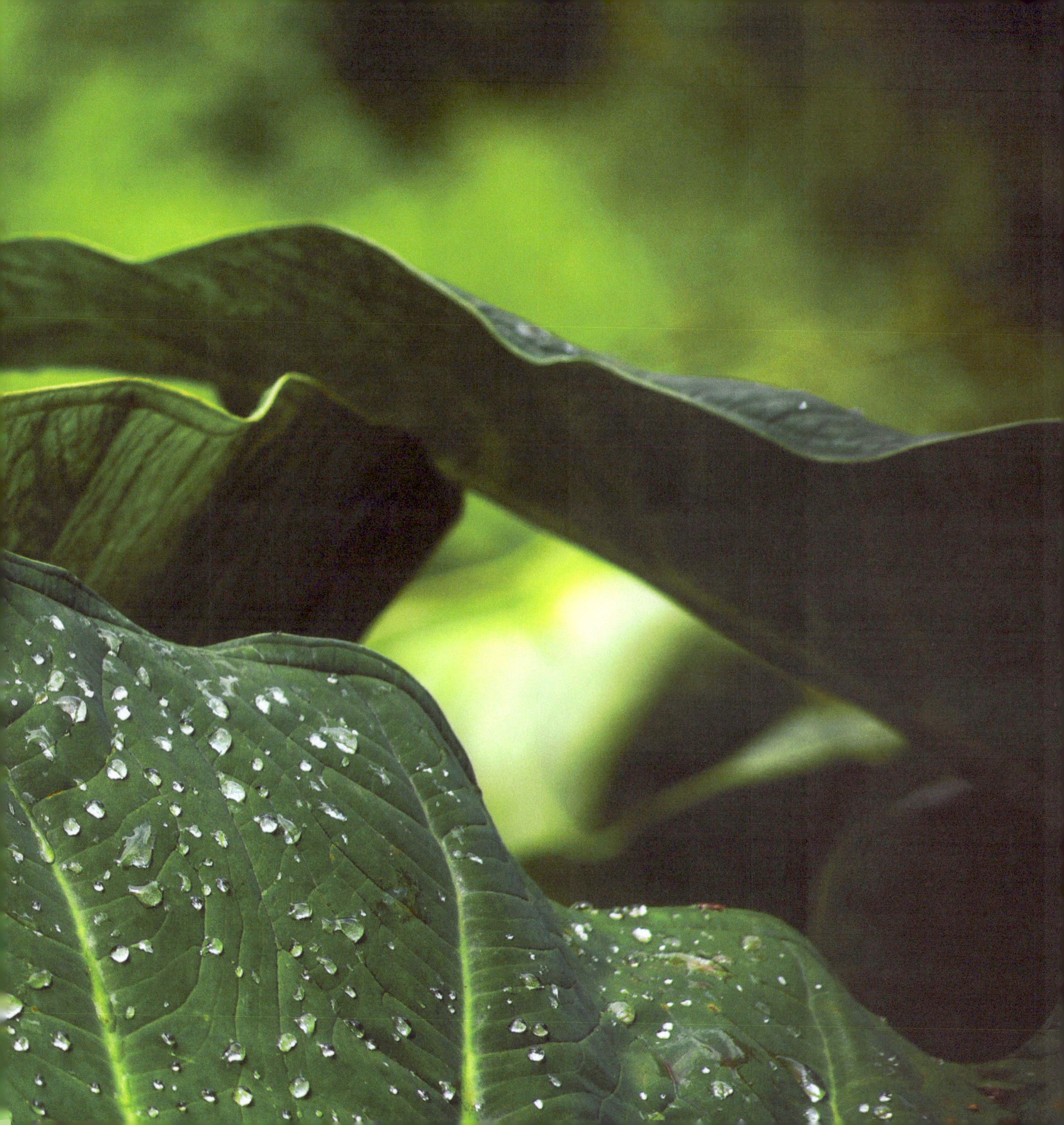

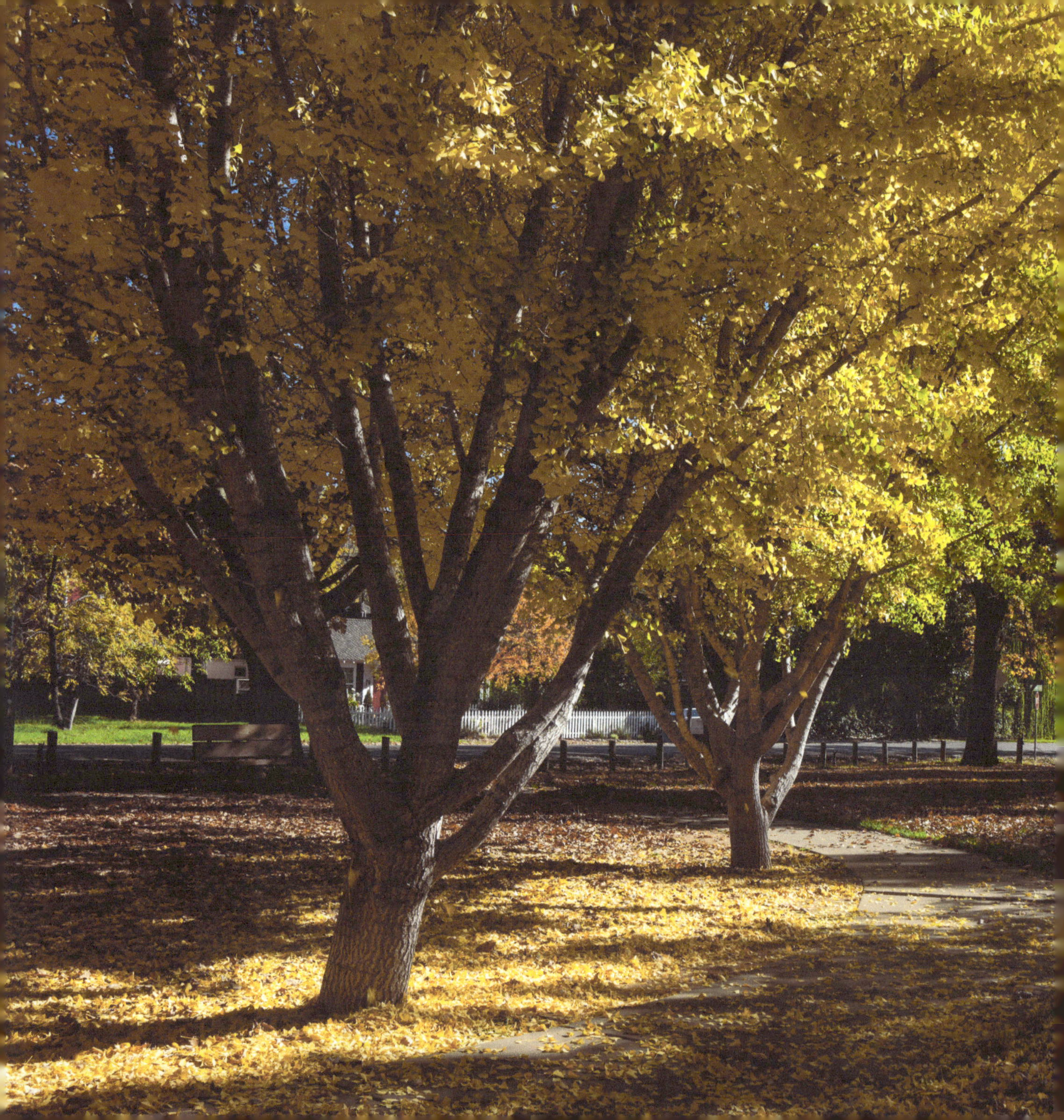

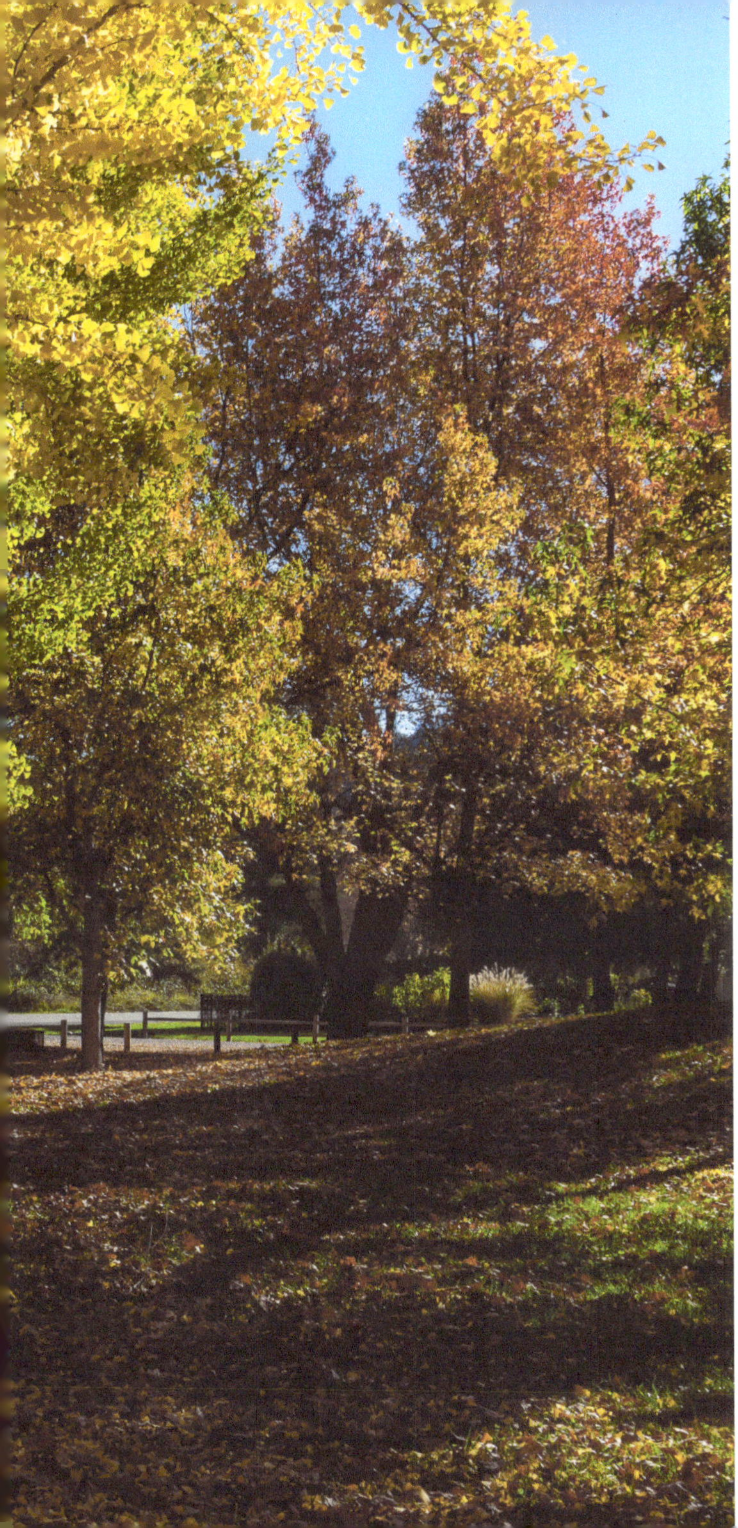

ACORN

A single acorn falls
Like the last pop of popcorn
One solitary note
Reverberates
The humble opening
Of Autumn's overture

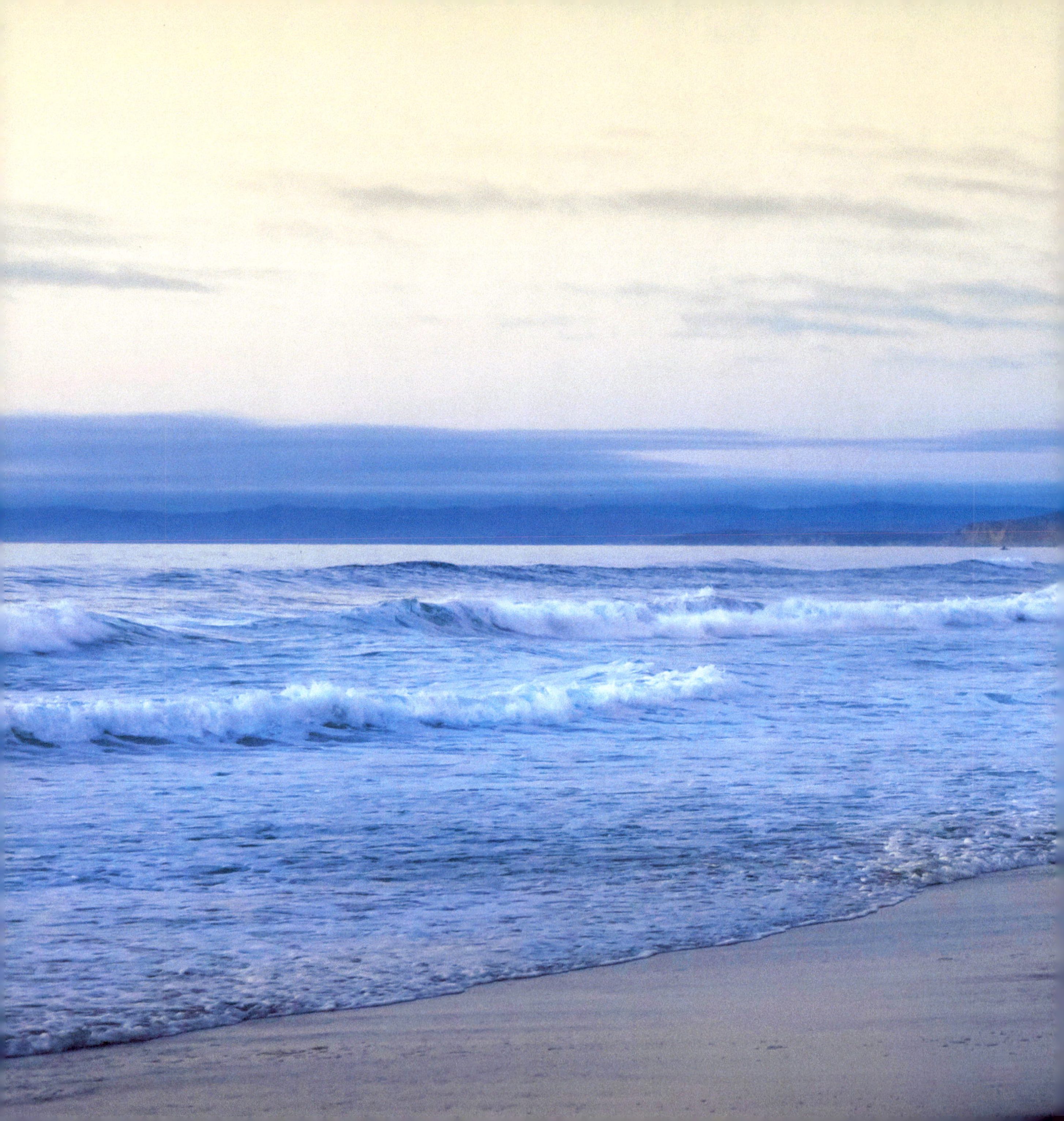

THAT SATURDAY MORNING FEELING

Everything is possible
On Saturday morning
The coffee tastes better
The dog is happier
The tin whistle
Plays glory
To the sun

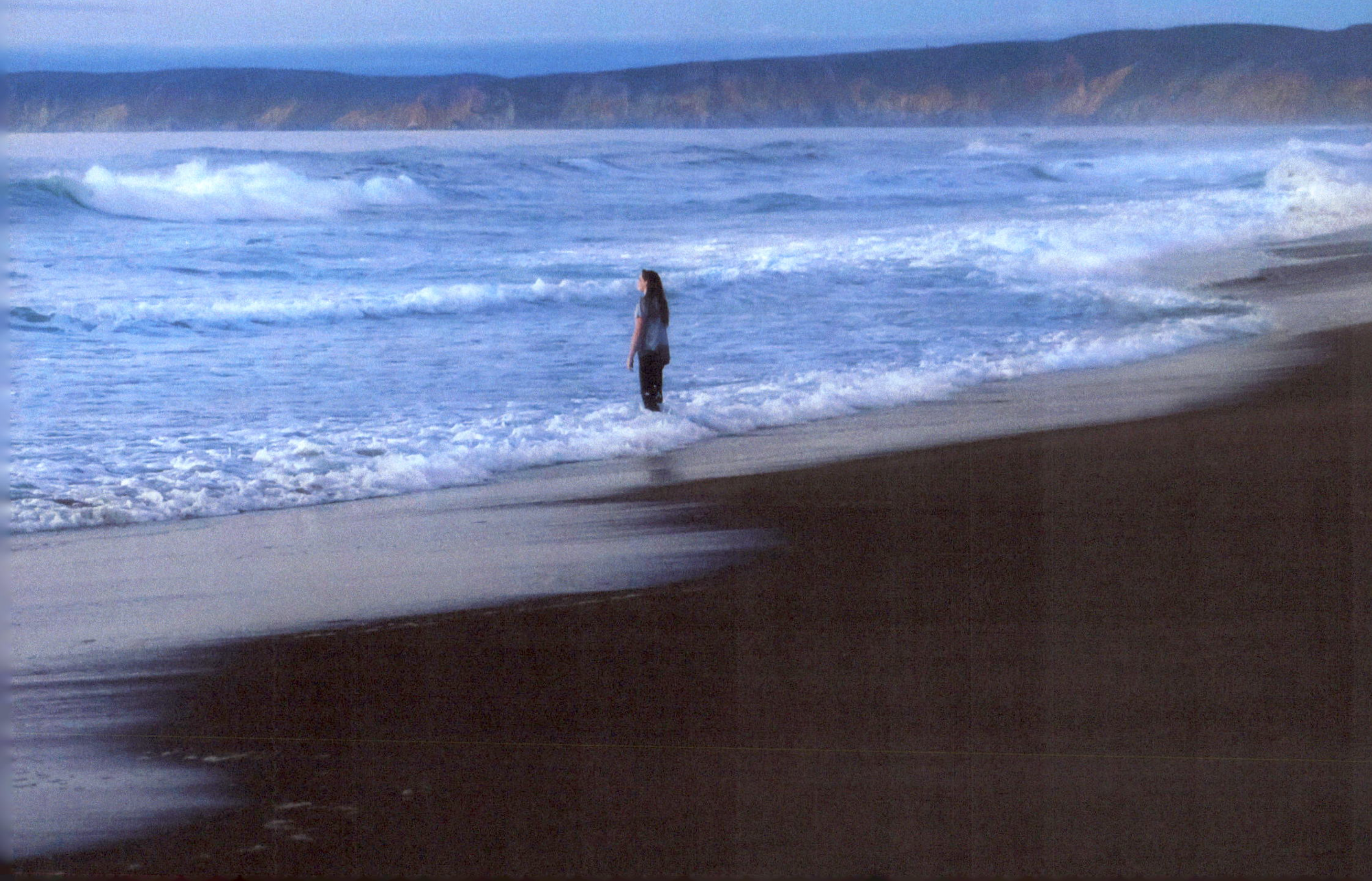

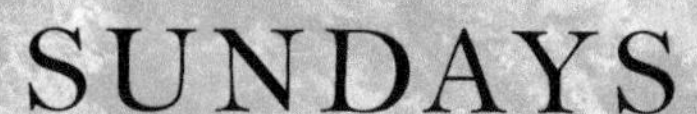

SUNDAYS

Sometimes I meditate
Sometimes I pray
Sometimes Let Go
And Let God

At times it's all three
It often takes me
On pathways to being
Inspired

The others nearby
They're finding their way
To follow their heart
Deep inside

On cushions
In pews
In circles
All views
Sit still
Holding space
For their guide

I used to hate Sundays
It felt like a sin
To roll over
And sleep
In my bed

But now it's a feast
Of spiritual food
To nourish
My heart
And my head

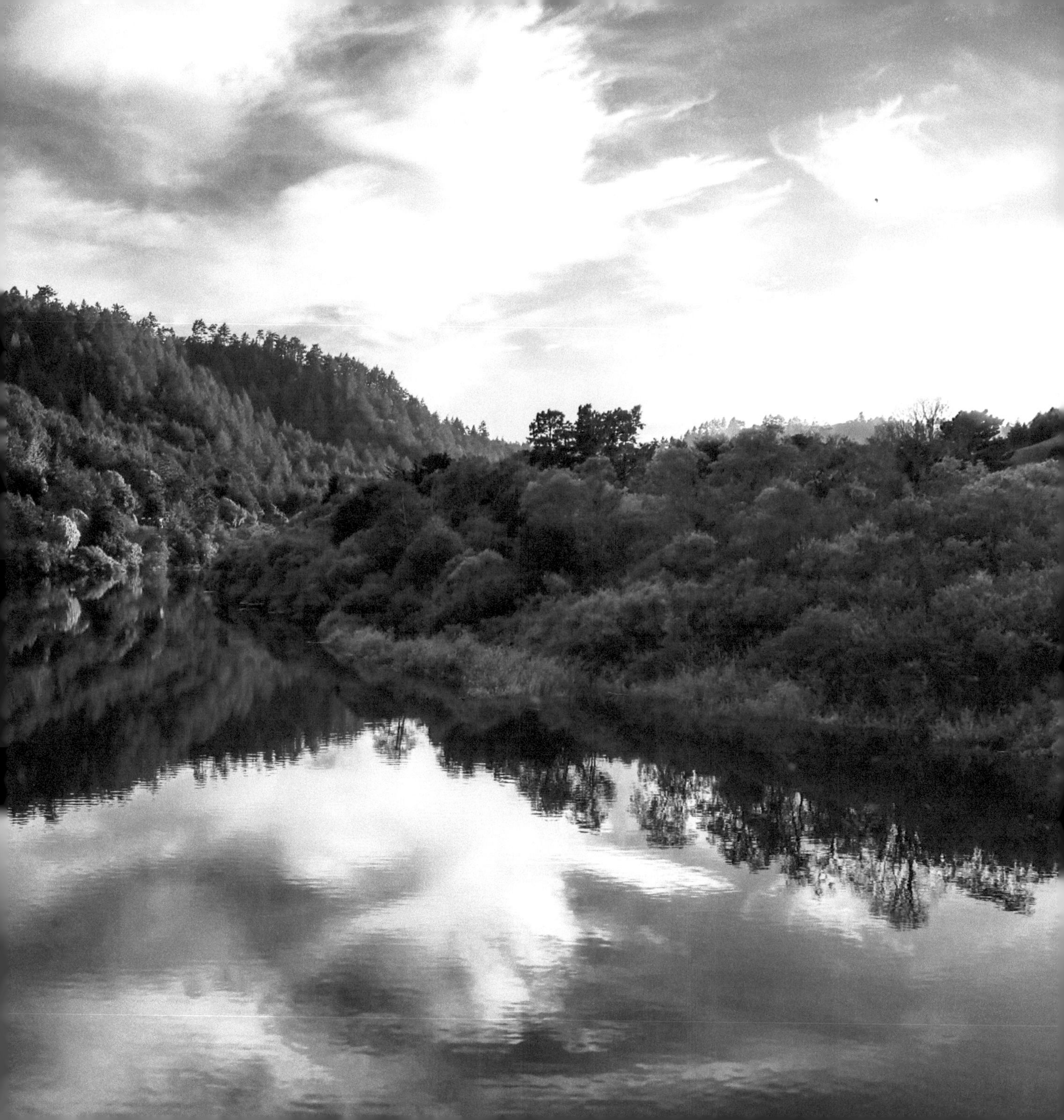

RED-TAILED HAWK

Watching him fly so high
The Red-tailed Hawk
Catches the current
Then slowly glides in wide circles
Through the sky

I see his streaked belly
His determined beak
His fantail spread out
Like a deck of cards
His wingspan stretching
Feathered fingertips
That touch the clouds

Massive, mighty
He sharpens his gaze
Slope soaring
Along leading lines
Searching for prey
And power

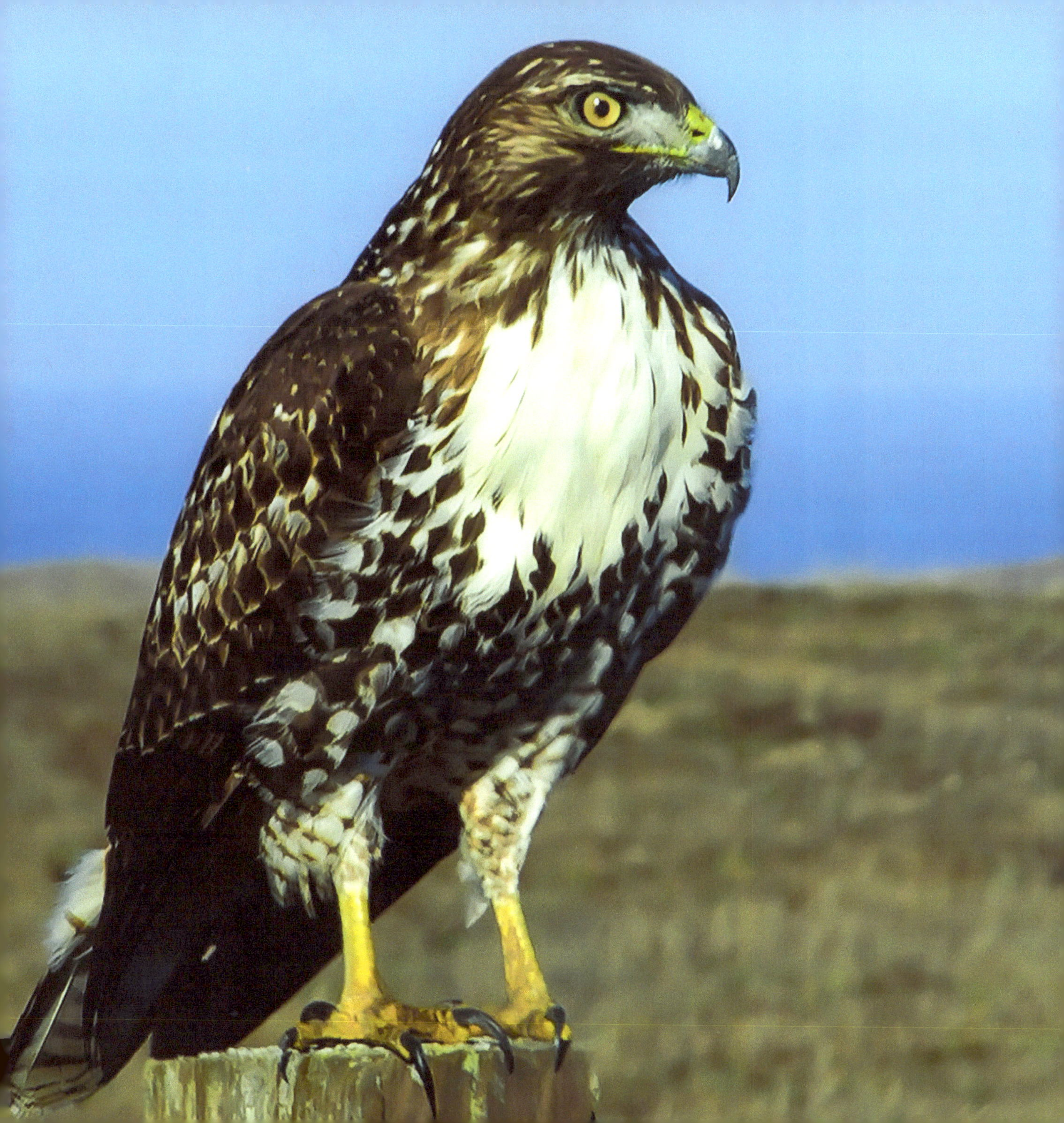

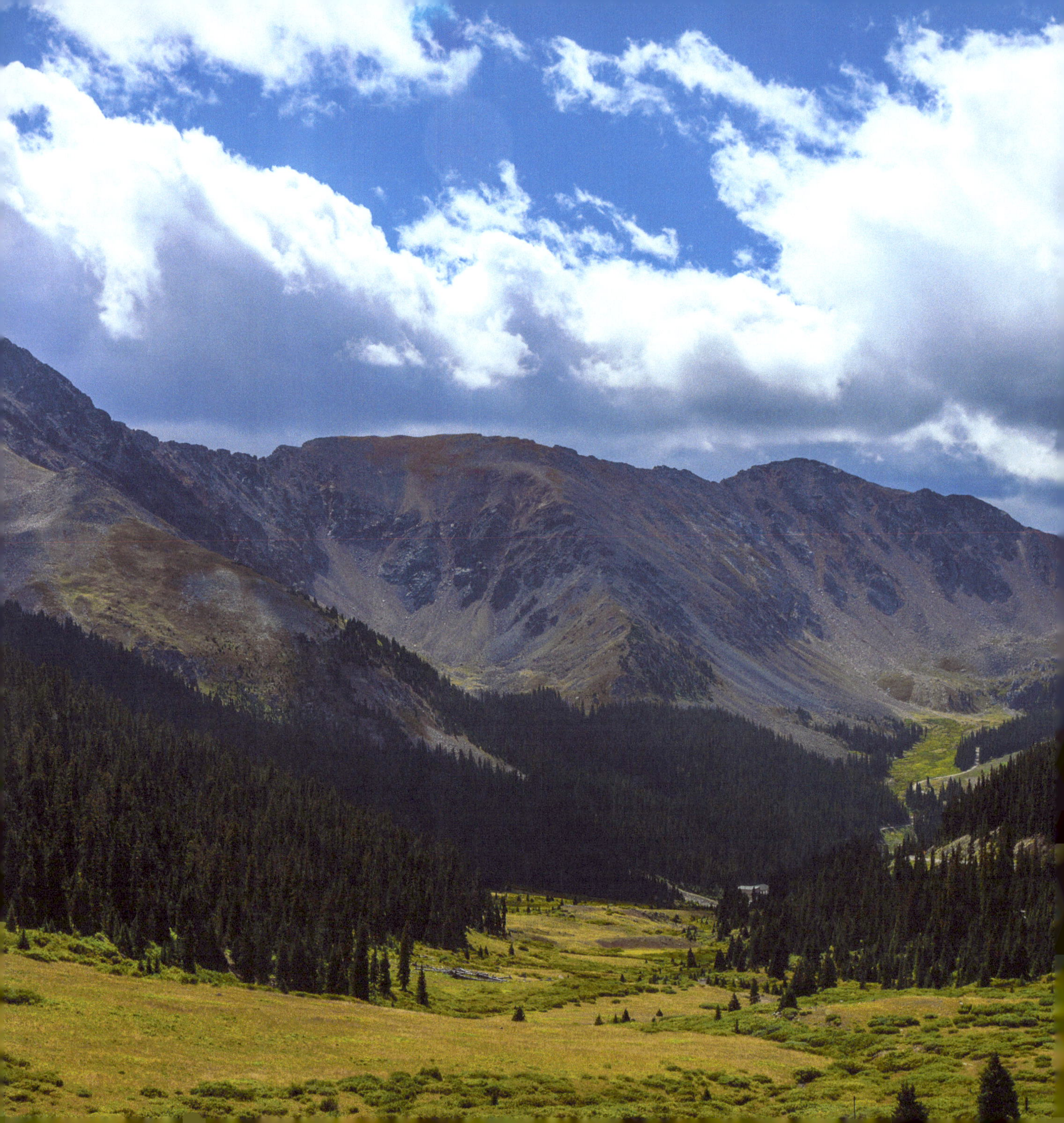

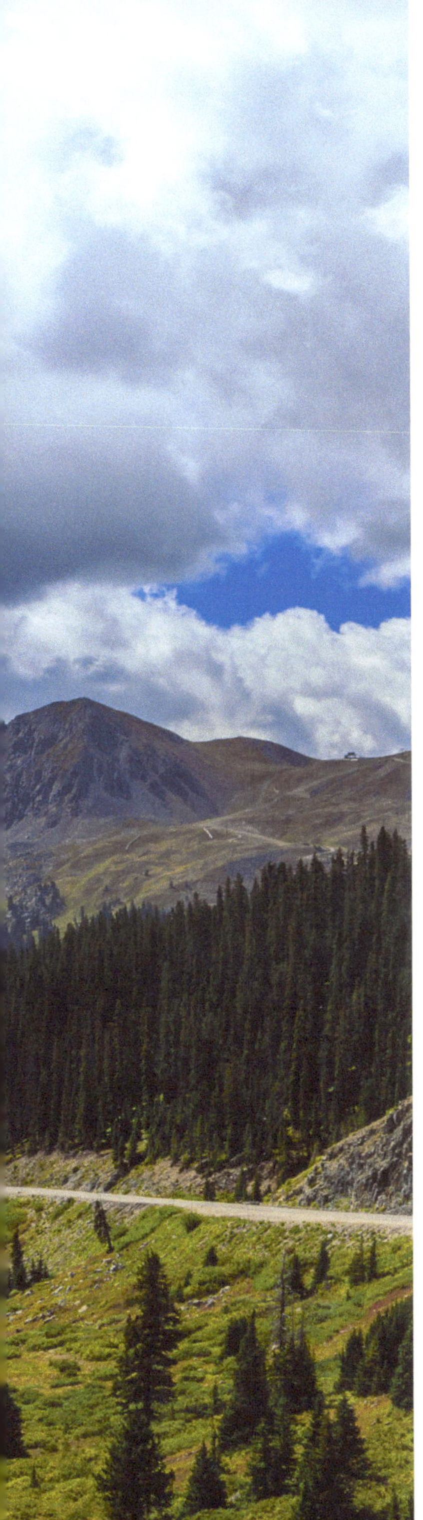

THE LOOKOUT

Trace your eyes
Along the ridge
Until you see me
Jutting above
The ragged line
Of Colorado spruce

I am the lookout
Searching across
The miles of time
For smoldering warnings
Or lightning strikes
For danger

I do not see
The aspens waving now
Their white bark fingers
Swaying back and forth
Nor will I notice
Their change to
Shimmering gold
As autumn arrives

I do not hear
The rolling creek
Or whistling wind
I do not hear
The herds of bighorn sheep
Bounding down below
Their coiled horns colliding

I do not feel
The daily sun
Playing with shadows
Nor sense
The rising moon
No lunar pull
Affects my pulse

I speak only
When danger is near
I sound the alarm
Call out the troops

I live alone
Hairs raised
For fight or flight

I am the lookout

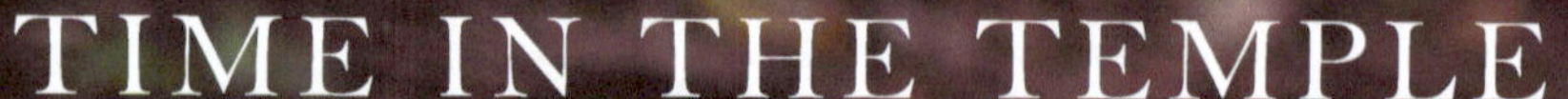

TIME IN THE TEMPLE

Time in the Temple
Atop Furnace Mountain
I am alone
Except for the birds
Whose insistent songs
Weave melodies around
My heart

But then I am
Back to the breath
My gaze unfocused
Peace filling my lungs
As the bullfrogs belch
Their baritones from
The lily pond below

There is space here
The mist this morning
Sits, like me,
On the mountain
Like a zen painting
Whose spirit speaks
The simple truth
That men are men
And mountains, mountains

And there are snakes here, too
Winding across your path
Flying squirrels
Gliding to the ground
And lunar moths
Lime green butterflies
Resting on the porch

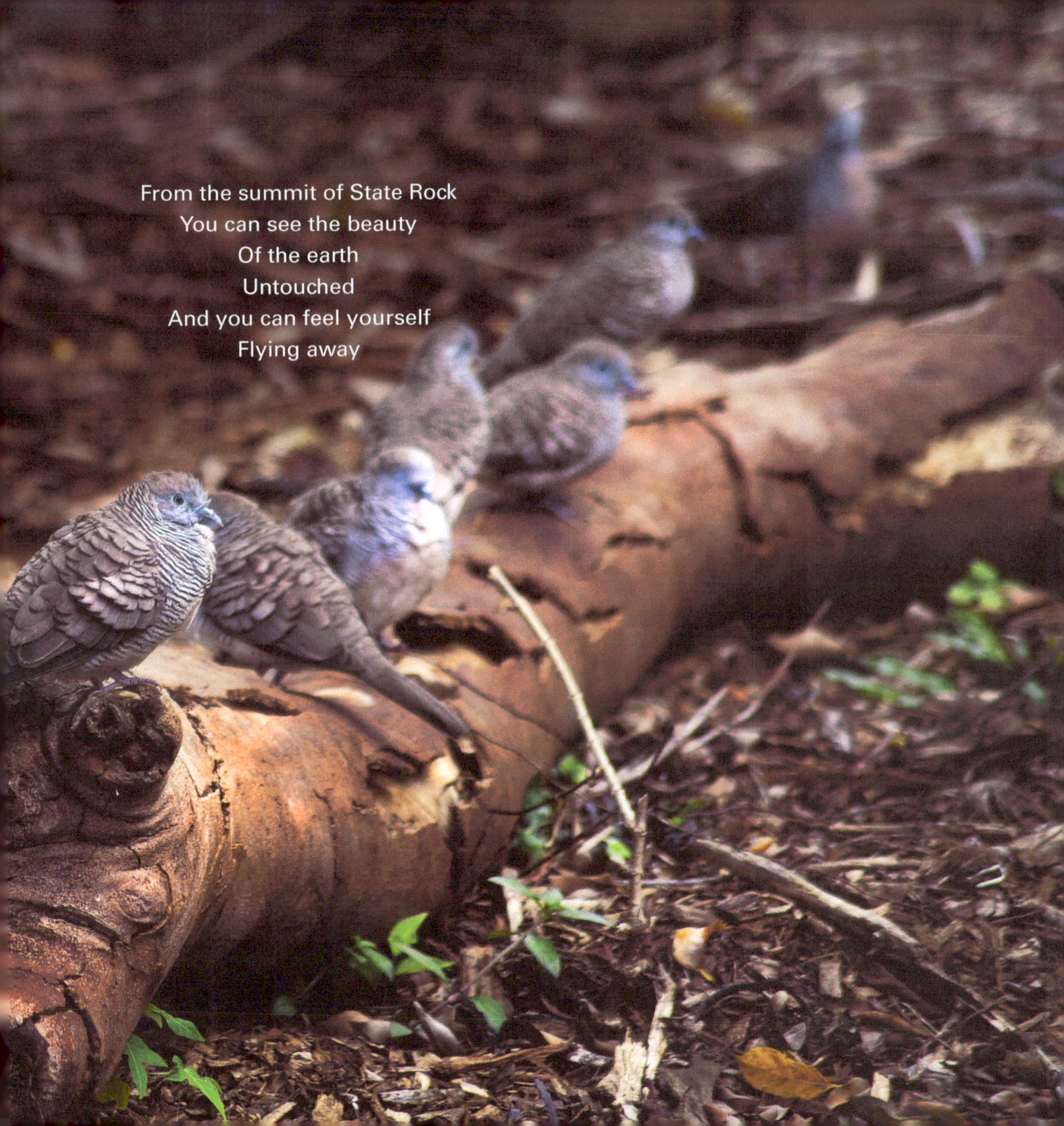

From the summit of State Rock
You can see the beauty
Of the earth
Untouched
And you can feel yourself
Flying away

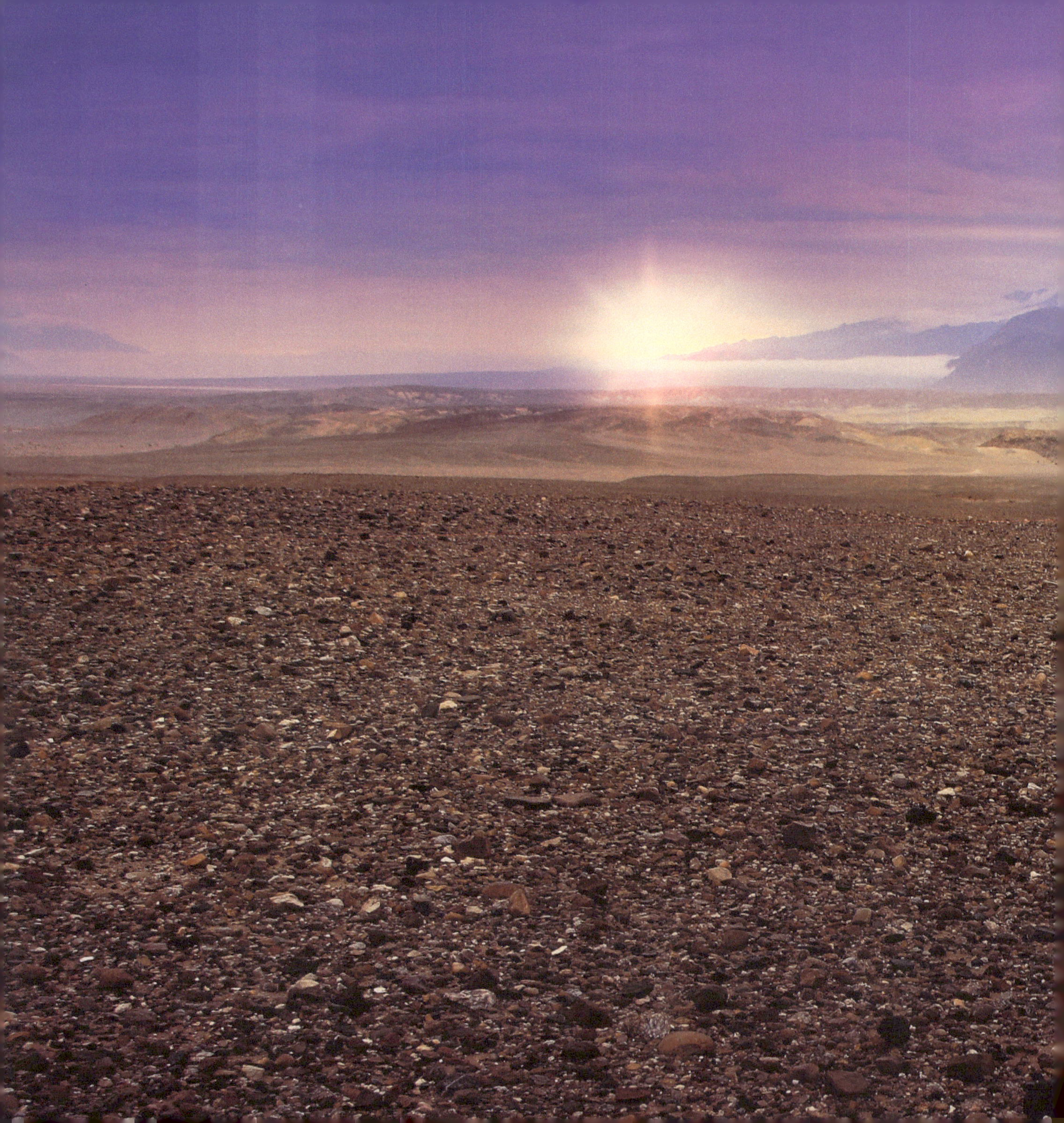

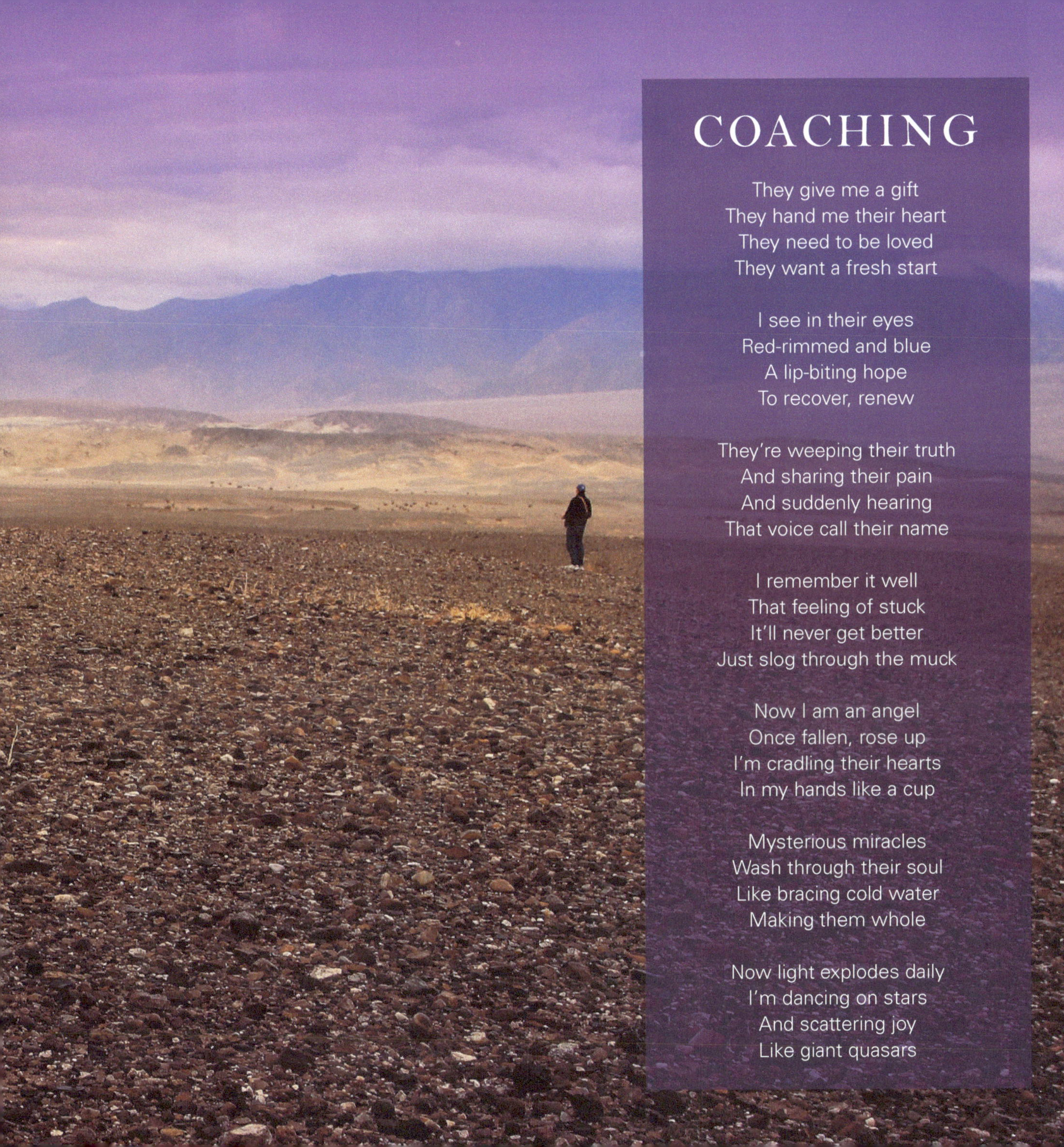

COACHING

They give me a gift
They hand me their heart
They need to be loved
They want a fresh start

I see in their eyes
Red-rimmed and blue
A lip-biting hope
To recover, renew

They're weeping their truth
And sharing their pain
And suddenly hearing
That voice call their name

I remember it well
That feeling of stuck
It'll never get better
Just slog through the muck

Now I am an angel
Once fallen, rose up
I'm cradling their hearts
In my hands like a cup

Mysterious miracles
Wash through their soul
Like bracing cold water
Making them whole

Now light explodes daily
I'm dancing on stars
And scattering joy
Like giant quasars

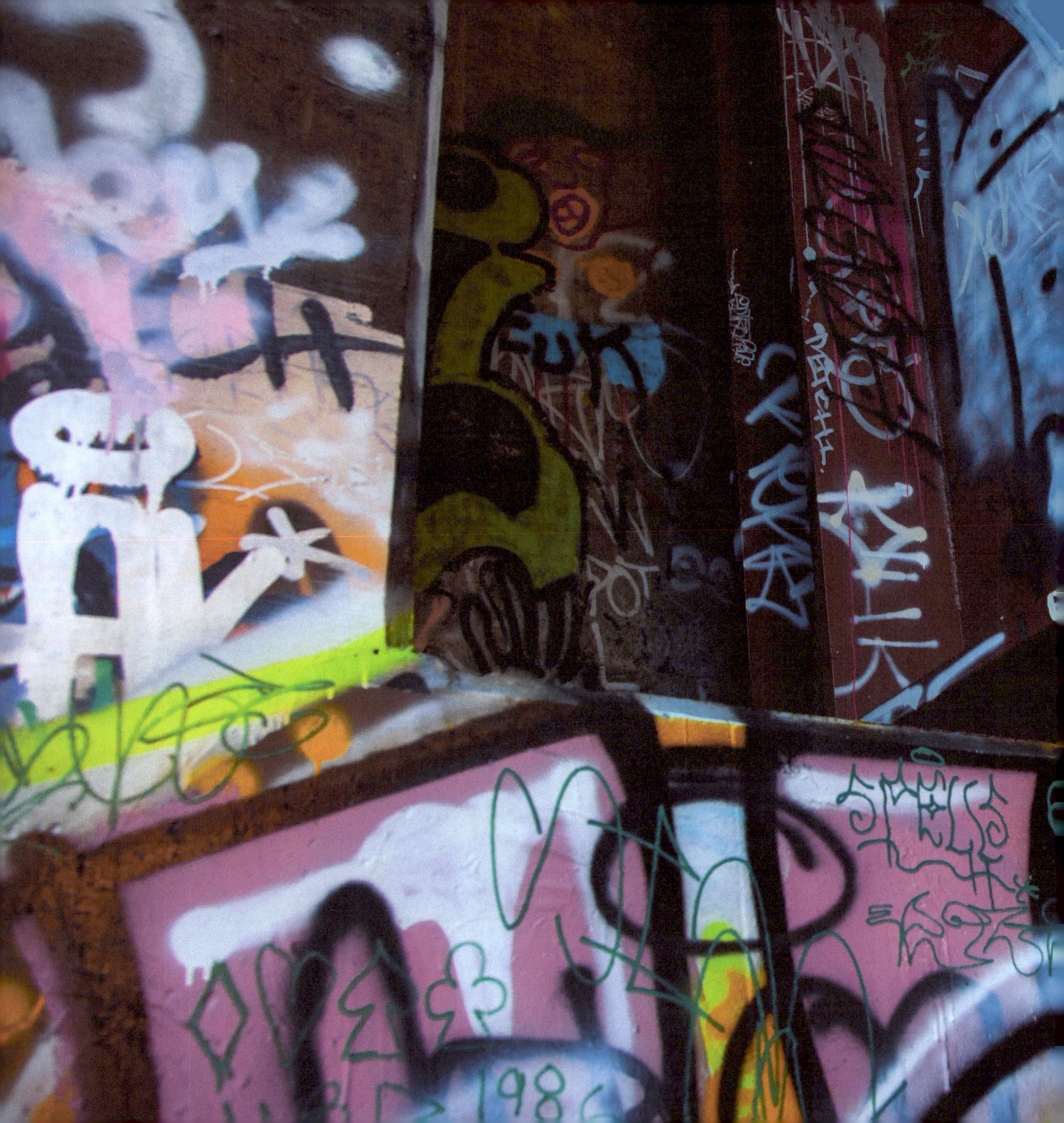

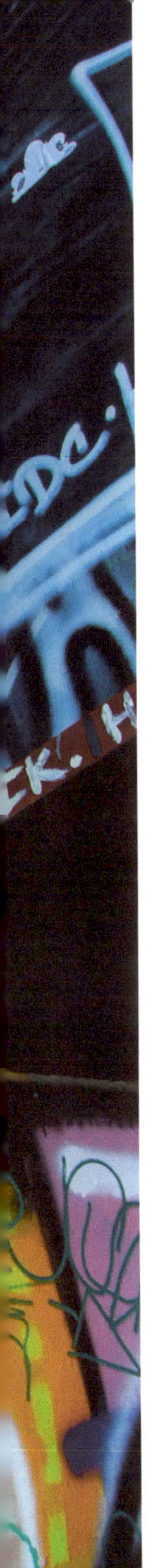

CONFESSION ON 32ND AND BROADWAY

I bend over and hand her a dollar
What's your name?

My real name is Julia
But they call me Princess
I'm trying to get back to the shelter

Let me stand up, she says
She springs to her feet
Cardboard sign in hand
She is young and pretty and sincere

I was born in the Bronx
Raised in Puerto Rico
We were drugging
Me and my husband
Doing the wrong thing, you know
Now I've been clean for three weeks

But he got arrested again
Friday
I told him not to do it
He's trying

But that got me kicked out of the shelter
It's a couple's shelter
So I'm back on the streets
He gets out today
We'll be okay
We'll get back in

She looks at me in silence
I say, I'll say a prayer for you and your husband

For some reason I reach out
Place my hand gently on her head

Julia and Jose, she says, smiling

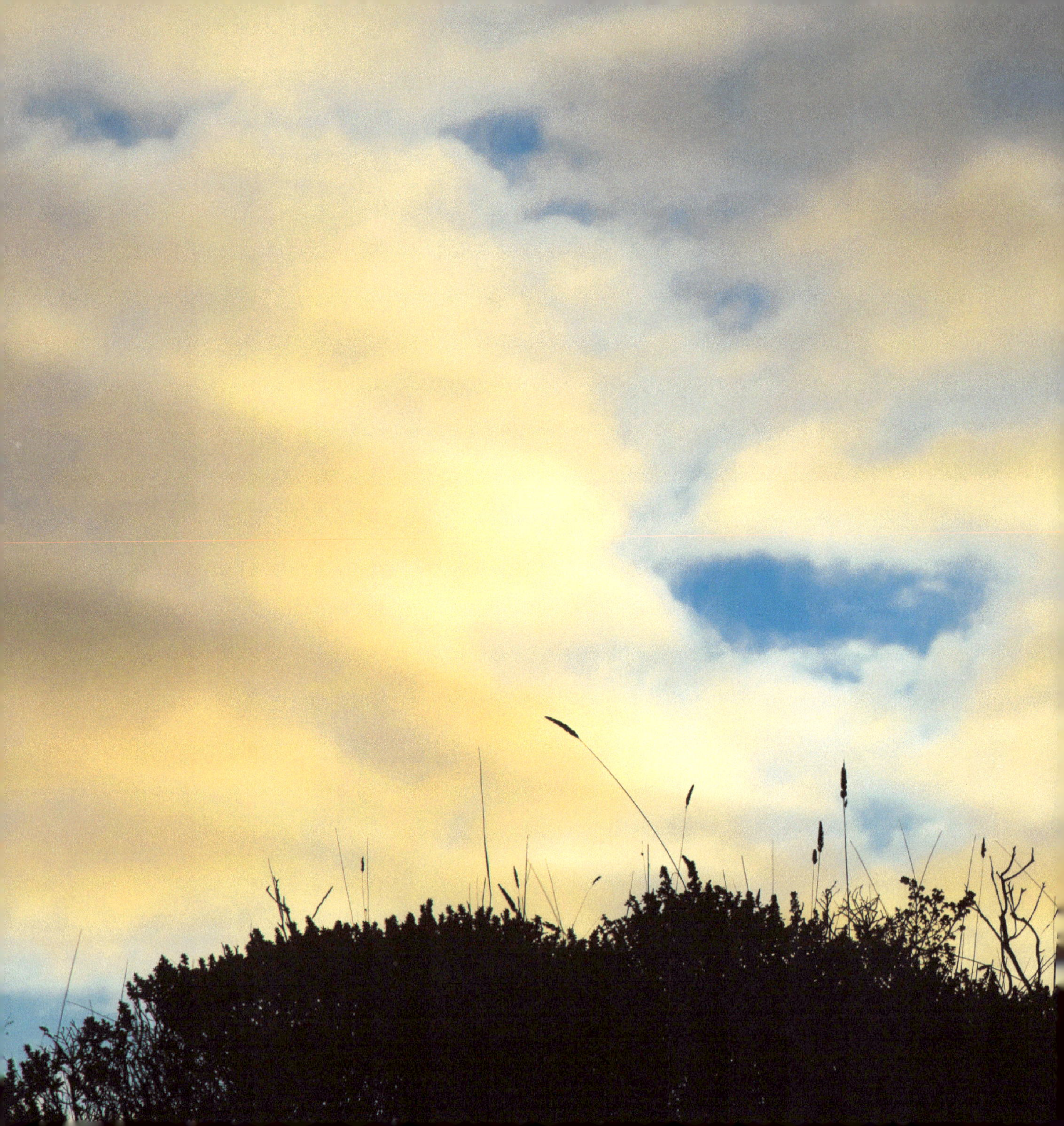

I AM IN YOUR CORNER

I am in your corner
Holding your crumpled pride
I steer you off the road
To solitude
To loose your spirit
In agony and fire

I gather your thunder
To hurl to your heart
In one magnificent bolt
Your unmistakable truth

I rouse your dancing soul
To the rhythm of the ride
And inhabit the margins
So you are not alone
When the taste is bitter
When the dark creeps in

I fly away with you
On beams of light
To galaxies of bursting stars
I blur the boundaries
That hem you in
Release invisible force fields
Whose gravity skews
Your soul's desire

I am a hawk
Soaring above the fray
Peering in to find your power
To call it out
Where you will feel it
Coursing like
The raging river
You will ride
To freedom

I am

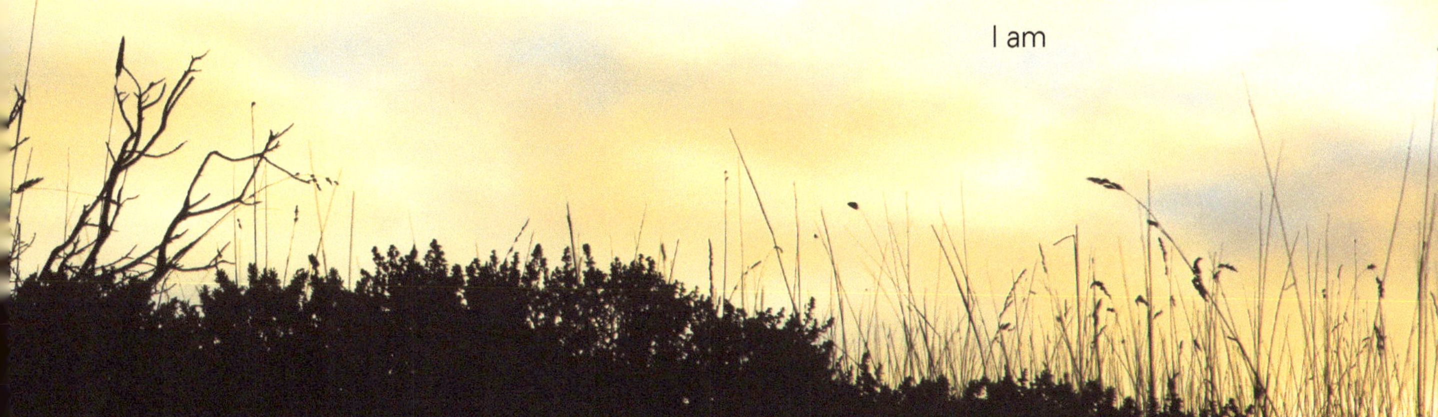

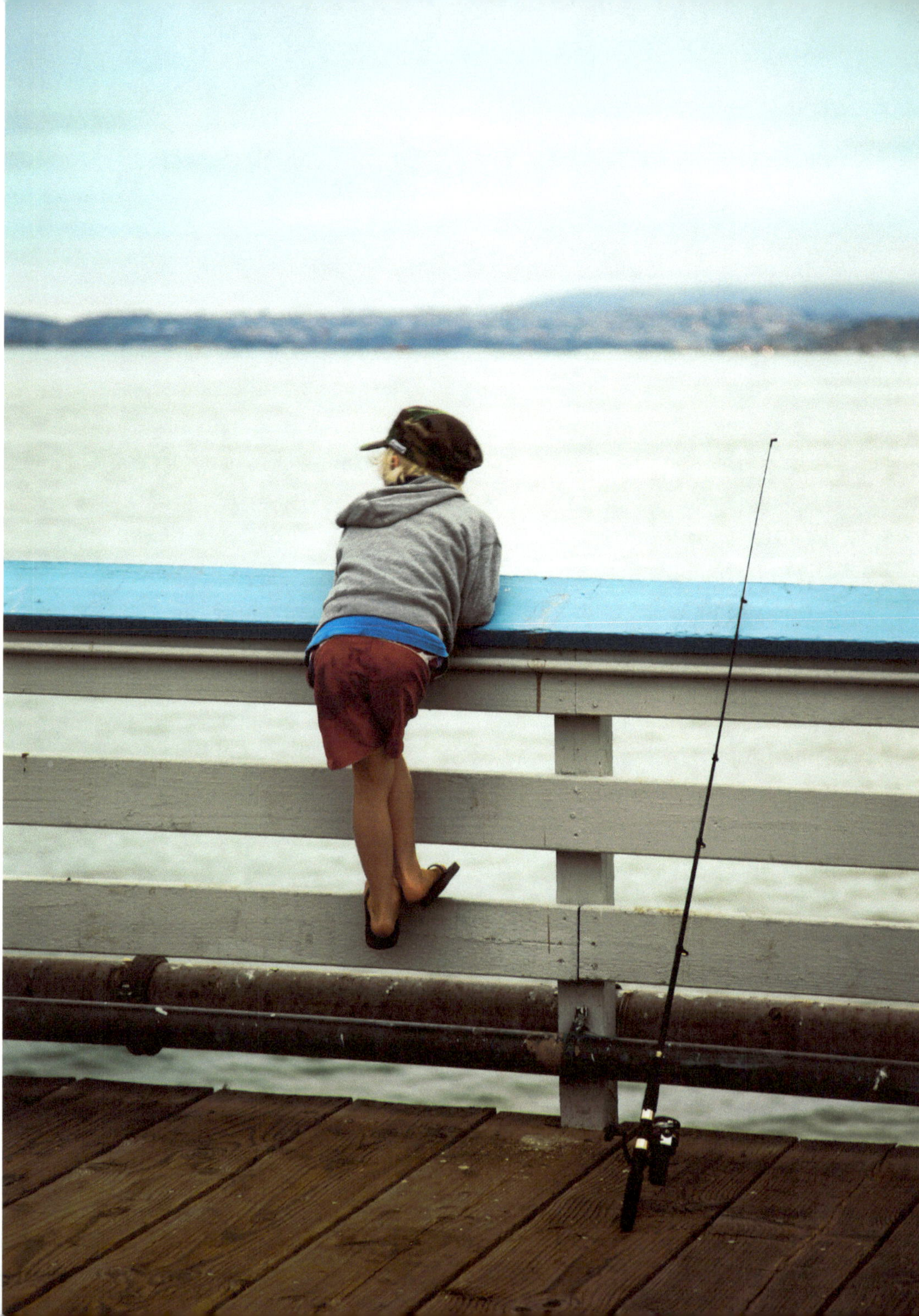

WONDER

The mother
Captures
Her little boy's wonder

His eyes transfixed
Dancing
With colors and clouds

She marvels
That such a gift as he
One day arrived

That he is hers
As each day unfolds
To hold and comfort
And love beyond words

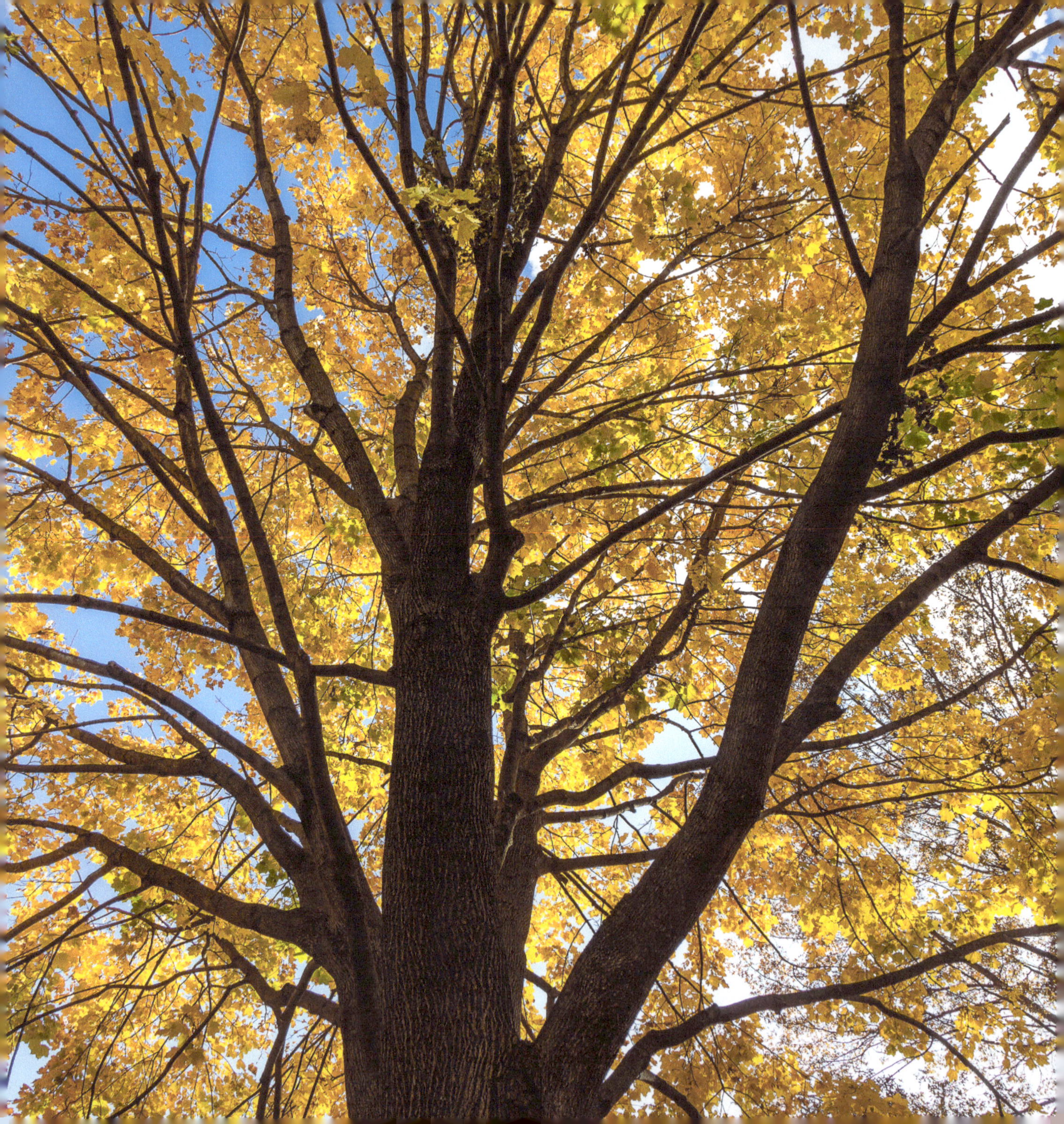

GRANDMA

Landlord's here, I'd say
As I crossed your living room
To climb out the window

You would say, Be careful
Always, Be careful

On sunny days
Like today
Steady on the pitched roof
I'd spray and wipe clean
Your big picture window
Taking care with circular strokes
To leave no streaks
So you could see clearly
The squirrels play
In our big oak tree

Now I climb out silently
No one to admire my work
I feel your absence

The kitchen we built you is long gone
No more cookies to sneak the boys
Before breakfast
I remember how that bothered me
But what were we going to do?
Yell at Grandma
For being a Grandma?

Soon the boys will be gone
More empty rooms
But for so long
Three generations
Filled this house

I put back the screens
Set the blinds just so
Blue October sky
Leaves spin down
I miss you today

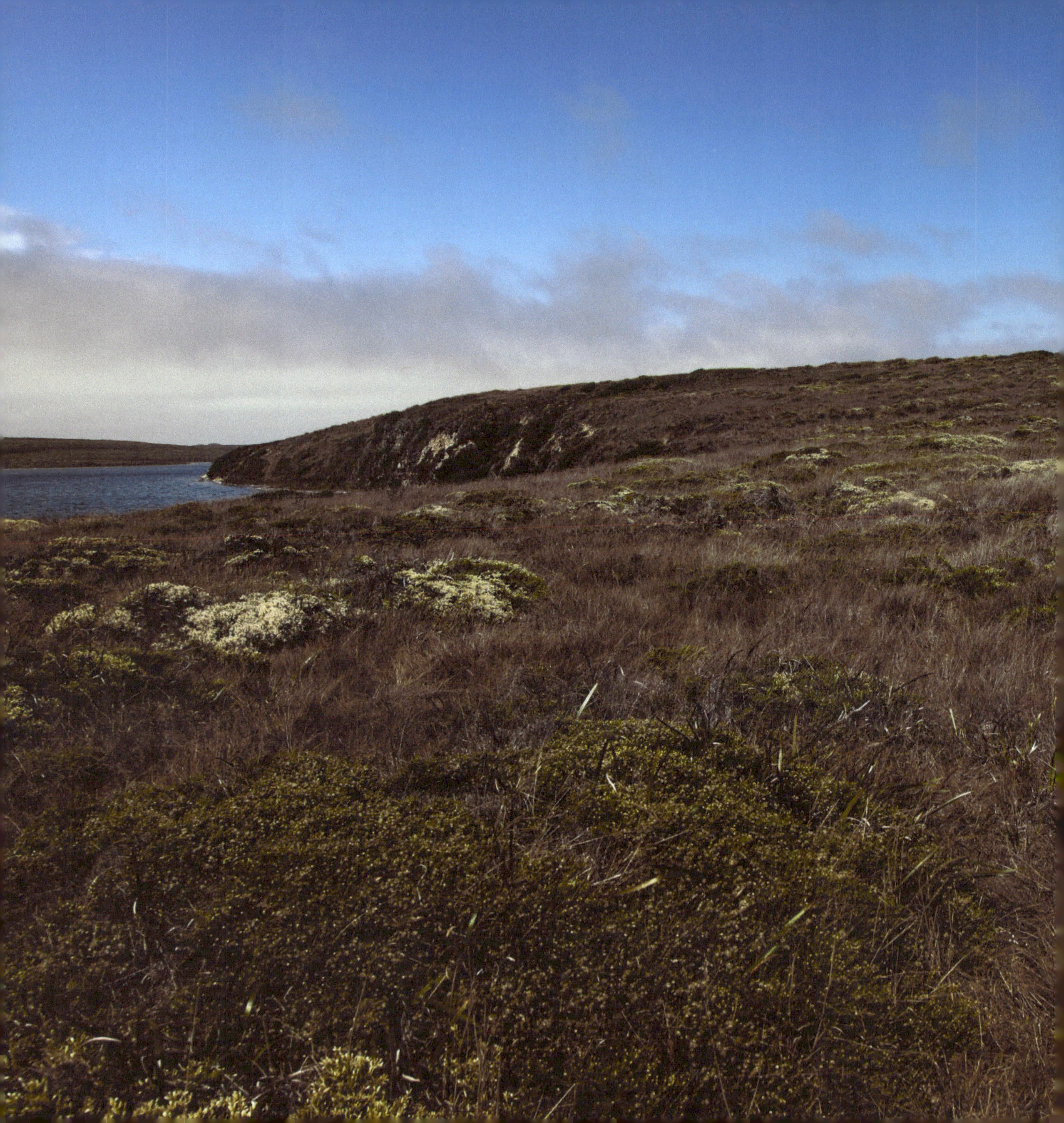

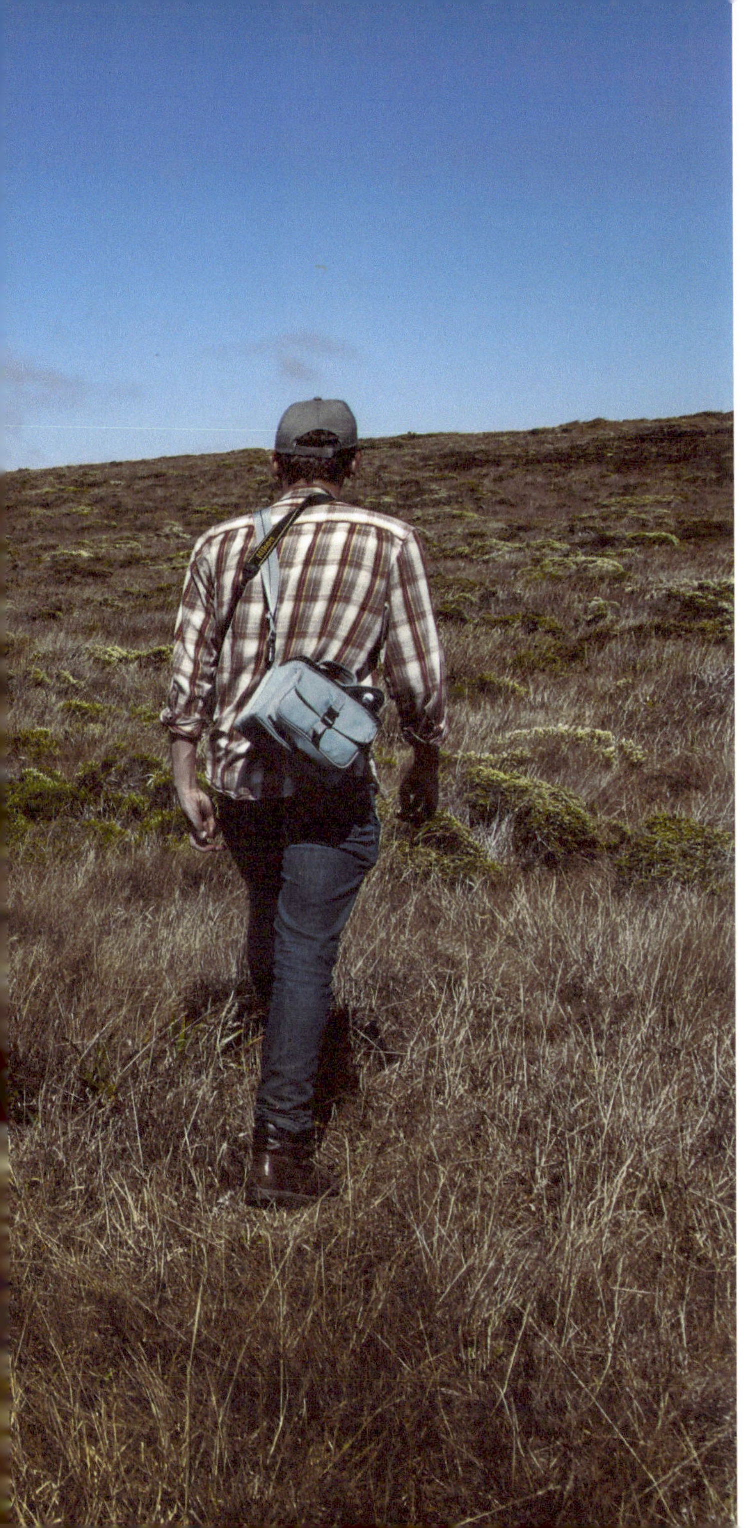

GOODBYE

At the airport
He reaches out his hand
I want to embrace him
He wants me to let go
I take in his handsome smile
A lifetime of moments
Tumble through my mind
I bypass the handshake
Clutch him to my chest
Like so many times before
Hold him tight
Weep
Goodbye

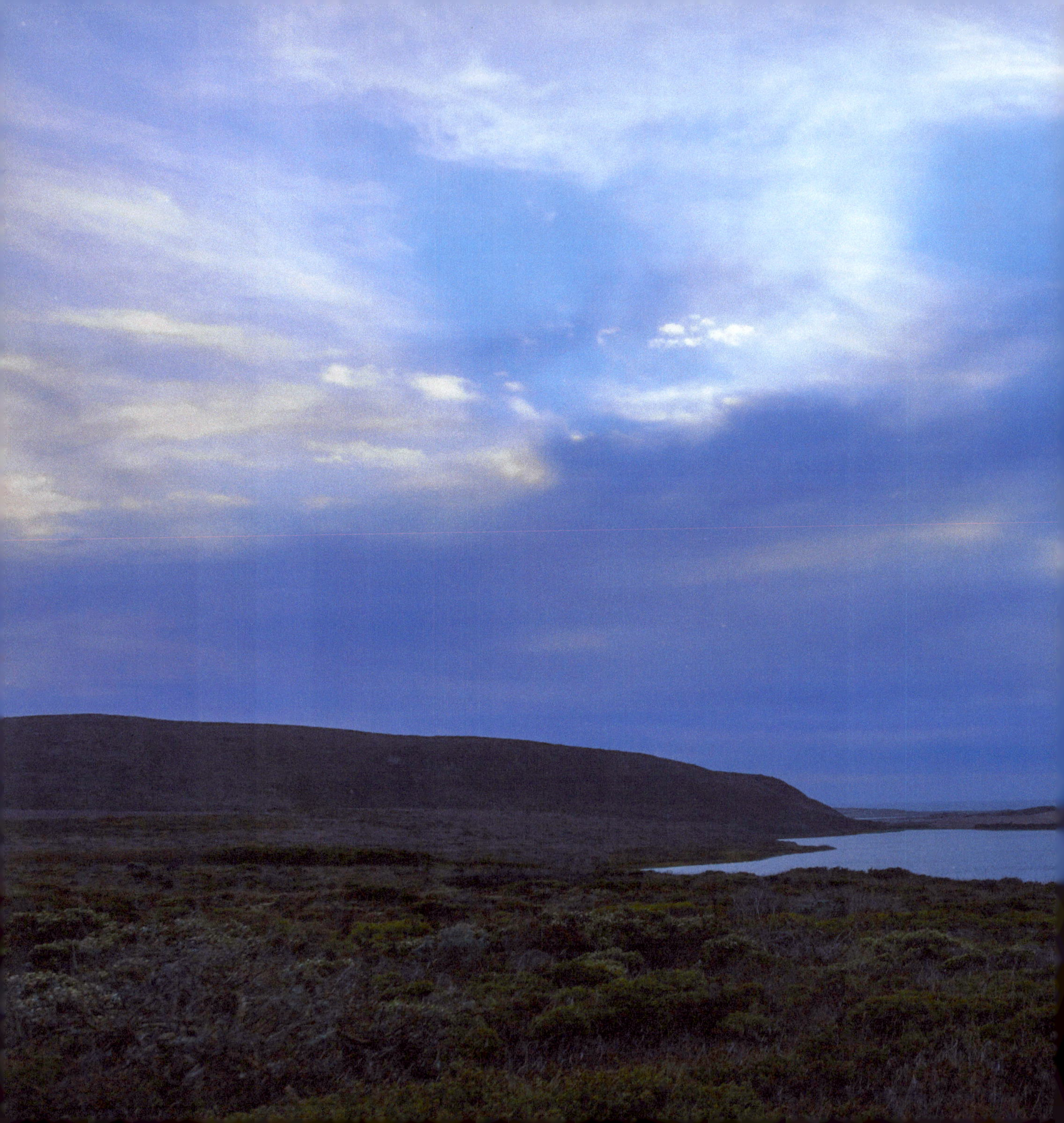

MIXED WITH STARDUST

We search
The great sky above
The sun of the day
The stars of the night

We pull our fingers
Though the soil
Dive deeply
The oceans inside
All to fathom
The meaning of our breath

From the dawn of life
We have walked this land
On all fours first
Then standing
Wondering
Pondering
Our place in this space

At different times
In different lands
We have received
The same wisdom
In different colors

At different times
In different lands
We have heard
The same words
In different tongues

It is all
The same spiritual food
Just different spice

The call
Is one call
Mixed
With stardust

The voice
Is one voice
Living
In our cells

It says
Love is the only way
Forgiveness
The only path

ICELAND

Northern lights
Slowly burn in
Breathing beneath
The wide and starry
Milky way
Sparking jewels in the night

Solar fingers
Flare from afar
This place feels like
The icy edge
Of the earth
A polar portal
To vast space

Iceland
Fade to white

www.ingramcontent.com/pod-product-compliance
Lightning Source LLC
LaVergne TN
LVHW071629100826
845154LV00007BA/116
9780986158544